Beat The RELATIONSHIP Odds

5 Essential Elements for a Vibrant and Lasting Marriage

MARGARET JOHANSEN, M.S., MFT

www.MargaretJohansen.com

Beat The Relationship Odds

5 Essential Elements for a Vibrant and Lasting Marriage

This book is being given to

_____

Because I care about you and your most
rewarding relationship possibilities

_____

Title: Beat The Relationship Odds
Subtitle: 5 Essential Elements for a Vibrant and
Lasting Marriage
Author: Margaret Johansen, M.S., MFT
Published by: Margaret Johansen, MFT, Int'l., LLC
www.BeatTheRelationshipOdds.com

ISBN: 978-0-9898200-2-8

P. O. Box 778296
Henderson, Nevada 89077

Motivate and Inspire Others!

"Share This Book"

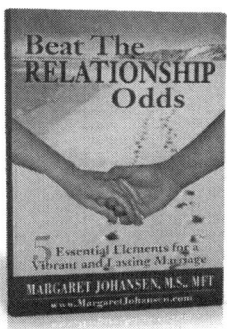

Retail
$24.95

The Ideal Speaker For Your Next Event!

Any organization or civic group that wants to enhance relationship compatibility among its members needs to hire Margaret for a keynote and/or workshop training!

To Contact Or Book Margaret To Speak:

Margaret Johansen, M.S., MFT
P. O. Box 778296
Henderson, Nevada 89077

702-492-6773
Margaret@margaretjohansen.com
www.BeatTheRelationshipOdds.com

Assurance!

The five chapters in this book and these exercises may appear easy. Some of them are simple — a tweak in perspective. Most are not! They require discipline and determination. I know this from my own personal experience.

In order for this book to work in your life, you must find your own Character of Self in the areas of: Self-discipline, Perseverance, Grace, and a Will to Achieve beyond what you have thus far accomplished.

If you really desire growth and development of relationship beyond what you have already achieved — read on. Please stop and actually DO the exercises. By participating in this process, the ability to accomplish the desired growth will be enhanced. Additionally, the exercises will reinforce what has been learned in each written section

Apply these chapters to your relationship life, and watch how your marriage and your life becomes more vital.

Contents

Acknowledgements and Gratitudes

I first acknowledge the formative influence of my dear parents, John and Lorene Arnold. Their marriage of 67 years provided a childhood example of dignity, respect, constancy, friendship, courtesy and duty that was unshakable. Their love for each of their seven children was shown in practical and measurable ways — my father taking me outdoors with him to help rebuild an engine or fix an electrical problem. When help was needed, it made no difference if it was a boy or girl child, whomever was nearby helped out with a project. I feel I acquired a rich education in life just being a member of the Arnold family! I am thankful, too, for growing up in a family of six siblings: John, Betty, Bob, Dave, Lorene, and Rich. We all learned to contribute, work hard, share, disagree, and work things out. In many ways, I still feel gratitude for the manner in which we grew up and grew together.

I express thankfulness to the man I loved and married when I was barely a woman, at age 21. With Trent, I struggled to learn the qualities of marital love, which are different than any other form of loving. We each struggled with the vicissitudes that were consequences of incomplete childhood development, that certainly were projected into our marriage. I have such gratitude for the development of necessary selflessness and largeness of heart, along with the rising self-confidence to uphold myself. I attribute this union as the seedbed out of which grew a vastness of my personal qualities of compassion, empathy, desire to understand others, motivation to seek ideas and solutions that would enhance vitality in a relationship. With grace and kindness, I am thankful.

Constancy of devotion has been learned as I have raised my five now-adult children: Trina, Matt, Brendon, Breone, and Heather. The depth of motherly love I felt as I first held each of them has never diminished—living as a significant portion of what comprises my soul. As adults now raising their own families and in their own marriages, they still demonstrate their love for me such that they are my most avid cheerleaders. The addition of five wonderful spouses, who have enlarged my family and my heart, has enriched my life and our family circle. The support from all through this arduous process of book-writing is invaluable. More expansively, their care and interest, connection even from distances where they live around the country, and sharing of their lives greatly contributes to my thriving in life. Spending time with family, which now includes ten grandchildren, invites me to robustly play, laugh, and engage, and care about yet another rising generation. My life is abundantly rich. An added special thanks to my son, Matt, for creating the visual sketches.

I cannot overlook the contribution to my life from thousands of clients that have entered my life over 18 years being a therapist. Every one came seeking hope: hope for courage, hope for possibility of change, hope for insight and understanding. Their vulnerability and honesty overwhelms me. They tell me and I believe I have contributed to easing their burden and helping them find strength and skill to solve particular problems. I also clearly understand that they have collectively given me more. From them, I have acquired a larger heart. I have gained an evenness in my experience of life. Because I know from personal experience that some people have lived heinous lives, my own struggles are made less burdensome.

I have little understanding on how either computers nor the internet work. But, I would be remiss if I did not mention my gratitude for both. I am an avid learner and researcher. Even though I still love the visceral experience of reading through a book, the information that appears at the touch of a key is truly astonishing. I have spent years now, using its investigative possibilities to enhance my learning. I have pursued a PhD degree, largely through internet interaction.

Thank you to all involved servicing this technology and making this happen fluidly most of the time.

Gratitude is also felt for the career guidance of James Malinchak. This book started out as completely a neuroscience text—one that would explain the conduit from neuron to relationship behavior. James listened to my ideas and boldly told me that my thoughts "made his eyes glaze over." He pushed me to write a relationship book, one that reflected the golden nuggets gleaned from a long career in working with couples. He was correct. This book would never have been written in its current form without his expert guidance. Thanks, too, for the expert assistance of Cindy, his sister and assistant. They make a helpful and expert team.

Lastly, I want to express gratitude for my faith in God, who Knows and Loves me. My church congregation and my faith are an important part of my life. I am grounded in absolutely knowing that I am a daughter of heavenly parents, first. And, with that, have a tiny spark of divinity carried within my human body. This faith allows me to look through eyes of love at the rest of humankind, knowing that we all are of divine origin. We all are just trying to find our way as best we can through this experience of life on Earth. I love having that perspective and the humanity it gives me towards all. God Bless us Every One...

CHAPTER 1

The Animals That Live In The Human Brain

This chapter begins with an examination of three animals: elephants, squirrels and rattlesnakes. Quite an odd combination of creatures, but they are exemplary of three parts of the human brain. It's a curious assortment of aptitudes, for sure; nonetheless, it's what we walk around with inside of our heads day after day.

The human brain is an amazing, amusing and sometimes annoying organ. Its diverse functions and speed of action are staggering. The thoughts and ideas that spontaneously spring forth on their own without a person "thinking about" anything are surprising and impressive. This mechanism of thought sometimes occurs without active incentive and can breed humorous results. Some of the funniest things people say are the one-liners that occur innocently, without conscious intention to be funny. The brain just creates them.

This is what occurs in animals, too. But animals have unique natural impulses and abilities that are exclusive to each species. We have three kinds of animal characteristics that both cooperate and compete within the human brain.

Elephants

Elephants live in fairly large social groups and work together as a herd. They surround their young ones in times of danger, strategizing against their predators. The young learn from the older elephants in their social community.

They have very large and complex brains that give them unusually good memory. They accumulate and retain social and ecological knowledge, remembering scents and geographical locations of numerous places for decades. They use their long-term memories to "keep score," taking revenge on other creatures—whether it be predators or another member of their community—at a later time. They have strong individual personalities that affect how they interact with other elephants, how another elephant perceives them and how well they are able to influence other members of their group.

These intelligent creatures even have been known to use their herd to form a blockade against a food truck traveling to bring supplies to workers in a salt mine. The elephants blockaded the truck and helped themselves to the food it carried after warding off the driver and his companion. It is interesting to note that, if they had had reason to hold a "grudge" against the driver, they might have worked together to harm the driver; but instead, they simply ran the driver off and enjoyed a meal from the food they captured.

Elephants develop a strong, structured society and the group follows the rules of the society that have been passed down from the old to the young. They model behavior in how they create tools, such as making a fly swatter from breaking a small tree limb, then grasping one end of the branch to provide an extended reach with its trunk. This type of behavior convinces us that elephants are capable of planning, memorizing, figuring out problems and attempting solutions, cooperating as a herd and forming strategies.

These characteristics are all similar to the abilities of the left frontal section of the human brain

So, to summarize how the elephant illustrates the function of the human left frontal brain function, they:

- Assess and calculate
- Make plans
- Observe and then learn from the older elephants
- Form strong social bonds
- Can work together as a group cooperate to accomplish common goals
- Discover problems and derive solutions
- Make tools to increase ability to problem solve
- Thrive on order and a known way of living
- Have very strong parent-child bonds

Squirrels

Squirrels are also ingenious animals, as well as playful and risk-taking. Squirrels can jump across branches in tall trees at speeds that mimic flight. Occasionally, they miscalculate, but they usually can salvage the situation by seizing another branch on their way down.

They are unbelievably agile and take risks by negotiating vines, shrubbery, telephone wires, branches, downspouts, walls, chains and ropes. They also have a keen sense of smell. Making thousands of food stashes per season, they rely on their spatial and olfactory memory to recall where most of them are located. They even are capable of constructing a decoy food stash to trick other animals into believing they have found an actual large stash of winter storage when, in reality, it is a small amount of food and mostly trash.

They've been known to paw at aging screens to enlarge the size of a tiny hole, allowing them to gain entrance. Curiosity and persistence are used in removing bent nails that were intended to be a sufficient lock. A squirrel will use experimentation and imagination to figure out how to tilt the nail at just the proper angle to remove it. Also, if you ever have observed a squirrel attempting to steal food from a bird feeder, they can maneuver around a lid on the top, bend around its surface to clasp onto a chain or wire from which the actual feeding surface is suspended, climb down the chain and enjoy a good meal on the landing where the seed sits.

Squirrels are one of the most cunning creatures, and are capable of using spatial perception to tease a tethered or caged animal by walking back and forth just beyond its reach. They are one of nature's most adaptable creatures, living in midtown parks or dense forests. Bonding behavior can be observed while a male grooms a female, much to her expressed pleasure, after she nurses their offspring. They also are quite frolicsome and seem to enjoy their ability to leap and jump from limb to limb with great agility, landing safely or grabbing onto their intended intermediate target.

Using their behavior as a metaphor for the characteristics of the right frontal lobe brain function in humans, squirrels:

- Can be teasing and playful, and use trickery
- Study a problem and then begin experimenting with solutions
- Explore many options and are persistent in finding a solution
- Have spatial perception
- Take risks and are spontaneous
- Are adaptable and creative
- Exhibit male-female bonding behaviors

Rattlesnakes

We have many preconceived notions about rattlesnakes, which primarily strike as a defensive measure. The rattlesnake has limited options for defense; they only can hide, slither away or strike out. The snake, being cold-blooded, spends much of its time and body energy trying to regulate its body temperature, so it seeks shaded bushes or ledges beneath rocks when the temperature is hot. If its body gets too hot, the snake will die. Therefore, much of the snake's brainpower is expended for self-protection and survival.

Rattlesnakes live a solitary life, so they do not form social communities. Only during mating season do snakes gather together in groups and may be found in communal dens. They have no capacity for bonding. Even during mating season when they do live in closer proximity to one another, no behavior of any snake benefits another snake. They serve only their own self-interest and survival.

After the normal gestation period, the female snake gives birth to live young in a protected place. Following birth, the female does not gather food or provide for her offspring in any other manner; the young snakes are left to their own devices to survive. Young rattlesnakes have many enemies and suffer a very high morality rate, because they are offered such minimal assistance for survival following their birth.

Rattlesnakes

When a human or predatory animal comes too near the hiding place of a rattlesnake, if there is time, the snake first will give warning by shaking its rattle. If not, it will strike immediately without warning. The snake also may try to hide or slither away, but if the intruder's distance is very close and the snake perceives a threat, it will strike. Although the snake may not be in any danger—often a human is not even aware that a snake is hiding in the brush and intends no harm—the rattlesnake perceives a threat, so it will react accordingly.

The rattlesnake reminds us how the limbic brain functions:

- Easily reactive without having full, accurate information
- Strikes from defense if it perceives threat (doesn't need to be actual threat)

- Has limited response options that only include fight, flight or freeze
- Reacts only out of fear of its safety
- Spends much time and energy in self-protection mode
- Has no ability to bond or form social relationships
- Does not aide in the survival of other snakes, only itself

The Human Brain: We Have All Three Of These!

The human brain has evolved into a most amazing organ. The human brain is made up of more than 3,000,000 miles of neurotransmitter pathways with billions of neurotransmitters creating synapses that produce thought and feeling. These synapses are responsible for bonding, using symbols and images, creating logic and reason, being creative and having fun, taking risks and exploring, enjoying music and art, and causing a large variety of emotions that can be felt at the same time.

Human beings like to think of themselves as creatures that display intelligence and creativity, compassion and warmth. We prize discipline that generates excellence in athletic performance and elevates those with exceptional mental abilities to high levels of corporate management. Movies that depict romance at its best are sellouts, because we want to have believable hope that we, too, can create such wonder in our personal relationships. We are visionary and principled, so we also want believable hope that our personal contributions will uplift and inspire.

All of these capable and lofty characteristics come from the frontal area of our brains that are most evolved. On the left front side (represented as the **elephant brain**), the brain has the greatest capacity to (1) conceive complex thought, (2) consider multiple aspects of a situation or problem at the same time, (3) express thoughts and feelings with language, (4) create order and structure, (5) use logic and reason, (6) name and label people, animals and objects, (7) form strategies, (8) be practical and considers the present and past using complex evaluations, (9) create complex emotions, and (10) figure out order and patterns. This is very unique in the world of animals. We have greater ability in each of these areas, because our left frontal lobe is larger than any other animal.

The frontal right side of our brain (represented as the **squirrel brain**) has different and unique abilities. The right side does communicate with the left side but has completely different capabilities. The right side relates to (1) finding the "big picture," (2) using imagination to fill in the unknown, (3) experiencing the present and speculating into the future, (4) presenting possibilities and ways to experiment, (5) being creative and artistic, (6) appreciating music and art, (7) perceiving spatial perception, (8) using symbols and images so it is more visual, (9) creating emotions of bonding, (10) risking and sometimes being impetuous, and (11) seeking the spiritual and religious.

If these two frontal areas of the brain were dominant in our daily experiences of life, one would think that establishing loving relationships easily would be accomplished. We could use the gifts of both the right and left sides of these large frontal lobes to form bonded unions. We could use the left side of the brain, the elephant brain, to form social structures and have the young learn from the old; work together as groups to promote the common good; solve problems by using the strategies that logic and reason provide; enjoy a large variety of feelings and be skilled at bringing order to those feelings. These are all the contributions of the left elephant brain that could promote a solid foundation for love.

And, with the contributions of the squirrel brain, we would be imaginative and have good-natured, impulsive fun; joyfully explore variety in art and music; benefit from experimentation and creativity in every area including career, sexual expression, spiritual involvement and practice, exploring relationship possibilities, enjoying the intense emotions of bonding, and envisioning what we might work toward in the shared future of two people. There would be fun in relationships and families, because the squirrel brain would assert its capability to be creative, take risks, experiment and try new things that sometimes might not work so well. Sounds amazing, right?

What Goes Wrong?

What happens when this often is not the outcome for so many people? What happens that makes the divorce rate for first marriages tip beyond 60 percent and go even higher in subsequent marriages? How is it that our very capable and evolved brains struggle to create meaningful and lasting relationships?

It's the **rattlesnake**! I won't oversimplify and say this is the only reason relationships fail. But it is critically important to learn that this part of the human brain has absolute authority in times of threat. Most of us never have had any education about this. It has not been taught in junior high school biology or physiology classes. It was overlooked in high school psychology and anatomy classes. In fact, very few even have learned this in college human relations classes or family science classes. Nor has it been taught in university-level psychology or physiology classes. We may learn the names of the parts of the brain and even the areas of function controlled by each section. But we never are taught what this *means* for relationships.

As the front areas of the brain have grown with centuries of time, the more primitive areas didn't disappear. The thinking part of the brain, the left and right frontal brain, grew around the limbic (rattlesnake) brain, leaving this primitive part deeply embedded and well-protected. It needs to be, because it is responsible for survival. And, it has done that job very well—we still exist as humans!

As capable as our rattlesnake brain has been to ensure survival, it is completely incapable in other ways. Like a rattlesnake, it is incapable of forming relationships. It is incapable of compassion or caring. It cannot feel any of the bonding emotions that facilitate love and sensitivity. This area of the brain knows only one kind of calculation: safe or unsafe. So when the rattlesnake part of the brain has been activated, and safety feels threatened, the only emotions a human being is capable of feeling are fear and, unlike the rattlesnake, anger. Nothing else.

The rattlesnake area of the brain only has the capacity to increase arousal, meaning it activates the body to become hyperalert and hypersensitive. Hypersensitivity suggests the activity of all senses is amplified and heightened for the exclusive duty of rapidly gathering information. The careful gathering and assessing ability of the left frontal part of the brain is overridden. Because of this, we no longer completely can trust the conclusions made in this hypersensitive state.

The body burns glucose at a faster rate, shooting this energy out to the muscles, which are immediately awakened into action. Increased arousal also generates increased blood pressure and breathing rates. Volume of the voice usually increases, as does the rate of speech. All of this happens because the rattlesnake has judged a threat or perceived threat. When the limbic brain determines an emergency situation is at hand, it hurries to provoke immediate action by one of three ways—fight, flight or freeze.

During such a state, we are largely under the influence of the survival part of the brain, not the relationship and logic parts, and it is at these times that the brain has a "mind of its own." From this limbic area, words can be spoken that later are regretted (the rattlesnake bit!), and behaviors and actions occur that do not help us achieve what we most want—lasting, meaningful relationships. We wonder who or what generated those vile thoughts, because they are so contradictory to the thoughts and feelings we have toward this same person when we function from the elephant and squirrel areas of the brain. The thoughts and actions even can seem foreign.

When the rattlesnake feels threatened, the instinct for survival overrides all other emotions that are created in the right and left frontal lobes. That instinct overrides the nature of our mammal instincts to care about each other and bond. Every other positive emotion that we feel in calmer times is put in the background, and survival instinct hormones flood the brain. Consider some of the emotions that immediately can be overridden by the rattlesnake brain, which feels only fear:

- Fascination
- Amazement
- Contentment
- Relief
- Amusement
- Thrill
- Rejuvenation
- Empowerment
- Compassion
- Appreciation
- Thankfulness
- Love
- Open-heartedness
- Engrossment
- Jubilance
- Generosity
- Invigoration
- Clear-headedness
- Fulfillment
- Safety
- Restoration
- Friendliness
- Encouragement
- Passion
- Proudness
- Refreshment
- Serenity
- Intrigue
- Pleasingness
- And many more

Another quality of the rattlesnake brain is that it takes in information at lightning speed, because it has lifesaving decisions to make quickly. Our elephant and squirrel brains work much more slowly in order to make accurate associations between various memories and experiences.

These frontal lobes try to make calculations about what actually is happening. Scanning the surroundings to take in this information takes time.

But the instant the rattlesnake brain feels the least bit threatened, it makes snap conclusions.

It has used only bits and pieces of the input given it by the frontal brain to come to those conclusions. It can't waste time worrying about accuracy. It needs to protect our survival, so it charges into action. It takes over the careful gathering of information done by the frontal lobes and starts hyperactive scanning, looking for threats. This speedy scanning now overrides the careful and methodical assessment the frontal lobes were trying to do. Once this happens, the limbic brain is engaged fully. At lightning speed, often the rattlesnake brain assesses too quickly to be altogether accurate; this kind of rapid assessment creates something similar to a fuzzy dream.

From the bits and pieces of information it takes in, the limbic brain determines only safe or unsafe, and unfortunately, it does not do a good job of determining what is actually going on. A good example of this is when you are dreaming and the brain is doing only associational activity without any connection to the real outside world. The rattlesnake brain reacts as if the suggestion of a threat is a nightmare, increasing heart rate and sweat production. And, like in a nightmare, you experience that you are actually in a place of significant threat.

The limbic brain doesn't do any logical analysis. It takes the intensity of the perceived danger as the truth of a situation. It is sure that it is correct and it is forceful. Once the brain has determined from its rapid accumulation of data that there is danger, it immediately locks it in. It can act within milliseconds, which is critical in an emergency situation. But the trade-off for the speediness of this reaction is that it cannot take time to process for accuracy, so the basis of this quick action is not well thought out. In making a snap judgment, it misses the details and nuances.

Let's take a look at what this might mean in terms of an actual relationship. In the Western culture, survival largely is regarded as having safety and companionship (connection). We are looking for love and the feeling of being cared about. It is common to conclude that if we believe another person is speaking disrespectfully to us, we are not being loved or cared for. For example, my husband might innocently ask me, "Are you going to work on your book tonight?" But within a millisecond, my rattlesnake brain might conclude that he is criticizing me for not spending as much time with him as he would like. Immediately, a sense of danger awakens from the depths of my limbic brain, and I believe he is accusing me of not loving him well, which seems like an attack on me.

The brain response at the rattlesnake (limbic) level is both instinctive and reflexive. Instinctive means that the response has been hardwired into our brain through genetic inheritance; it is not learned. Reflexive is when a stimulus happens, a response occurs automatically. Because it is an automatic response, it also is largely unregulated, which is why we feel fear or anger immediately with such enormous intensity. These emotions are likely to be far more exaggerated than for what the situation calls.

Once the limbic brain has perceived a threat, the production of stress hormones begins. Particularly in the frontal lobes of the brain, the stress hormones change the biochemical "soup" that the neurotransmitters need to function within, and they begin to have a more difficult time doing their job. If they don't connect, we cannot think clearly. This can occur with lightning speed, or it can occur gradually. In either case, our ability to reason and problem solve is compromised. Our ability to listen without distortion is clearly put at risk. It becomes difficult to hold a steady connection to the other person due to these increased levels of stress hormones that have flooded the thinking and bonding frontal lobes (elephant and squirrel).

In short, when a threat or perceived threat activates the limbic brain, it compromises our ability to function as a thinking and feeling mammal. Then we are subject to a much less evolved brain; one that concerns itself only with survival, rather than the emotions of love or caring.

Now, even in doing the best thinking it can, the thought process of the frontal lobes, which have become flooded with stress hormones, is going to be distorted. So it more often is overwhelmed in the experience of the rattlesnake, which is fight, runaway or freeze.

All of us have experienced this. Every time I explain this cycle to clients, a light comes on in their mind. They typically say, "I can absolutely *feel* when this happens! I know just what you are talking about." And they also say, "Why did they not teach this to me in junior high? It would have made such a difference!"

When we feel a strong surge that urges us to formulate instant criticism toward a person who, under normal circumstances we know we care about, we have entered our limbic brain. When we feel a very strong urge to just blurt out our thoughts and feelings instead of listening to and understanding another, we have entered the limbic brain. When we feel unable to keep our own emotions steady, while a spouse or child is expressing strong emotion, we probably have entered our limbic brain. Also, when we feel a strong, physical impulse to lash out and hurt someone we care about, we are experiencing the fighting impulse that comes from the limbic brain. In moments like this, the hardwired programming that exists in every human being is activated, so you fight, flight or freeze up. This survival part of our brain cannot think, work anything out or care about the other person involved. It cannot perform any of the functions of which the higher-level thinking areas of the brain are capable—it only can help us survive.

So that you can better identify when you are under the rule of the limbic survival functions, let's take a look at what might happen in each of the possible defense responses of this part of the brain: fight, flight and freeze.

FIGHT: The reptilian response to fight takes many forms in relationships. Fighting is one person doing something that will intentionally cause pain or distress for another. Rapidly elevated speech, higher or lower pitch in voice, and increase in volume and intensity all suggest fight. Additionally, the characteristic tension in the muscles, frown of the brow and terse look in the eyes also are experienced as the limbic sends the command to fight. This typically involves blaming, criticizing, yelling or being physically aggressive. What couples describe as arguments are most likely expressive of the rattlesnake brain in control. In response, often the receiver mirrors the behavior and the two "rattlesnakes" battle for dominance or survival.

FLIGHT: To flee means attempting to create distance between you and a perceived threat. The obvious physical way to do this is to run or drive away. But in actuality, we accomplish this distance in many ways.

Margaret Johansen, M.S., MFT

An entire chapter could be written on couples' behaviors that create distance, both intentionally and unintentionally. Some of the ways that couples may attempt to ward off connection might be:

- Tuning out each other by watching TV
- Becoming absorbed in a romance novel or other reading specifically to avoid interaction with the other
- Avoiding eye contact or ignoring
- Staying after-hours at work to avoid going home
- Initiating a very long phone call with someone else to avoid connection with their partner
- Exaggerating time needed at the computer or other electronic devices
- Changing the subject

FREEZE: The retina of most wild animals is programmed to detect movement, because a predator sneaking closer eventually will attack. To the rattlesnake brain, movement can cause death. In relationships, being silent and still is an attempt to become invisible. The most common way we create freezing, or paralysis, is to be physically present but emotionally shut down. Ignoring questions is a means of freezing. Because telling the truth is determined not to be safe, lying also is often the limbic brain doing its job to keep the person safe, just as is an attempt to freeze and avoid.

The Prefrontal Cortex
(Thinking Brain) Solution To This Problem

You may be thinking that the description of this hardwiring presents an insolvable problem. You may be right! If you don't learn how to override the natural impulses of the limbic brain, it can create unsolvable relational problems. The hardwiring we have inherited is very compelling, and it is capable of causing major disruption in a relationship. You cannot force the impulse of the rattlesnake brain not to happen, but you can override it. With practice, you can learn to work with your inner rattlesnake in a way that supports the real desires of the prefrontal cortex, which is long-term love and intimacy.

There are two primary skills that will help you manage the impulses of the limbic brain. One of those is a completely internal process, meaning that you work exclusively with your own thoughts and impulses. To do this, specific language is recommended with a precise process that ensures success. I have named this The Observer.

The Observer

Imagine that your emotions have just escalated abruptly. You experience the impulses of fight, flight or freeze. Immediately, you call upon The Observer, which is a resource you have within yourself. You can imagine the Observer as a layer of your own mature adult self. It is neutral, unaroused and competent to figure out what is actually occurring. The Observer wants to integrate the brain with heartfelt feeling once again, but experience has informed it to first discover what is occurring in this very moment.

The Observer lives inside of your head. This dutiful sleuth has a job to do, and is very detailed and specific about what that job is and how it should be done. If The Observer is allowed the opportunity to do its work, the result will be successful bridling of intense emotional reactions.

The directions to access The Observer are as follows:

1. As soon as the elevated impulse is felt, pay attention to it. Observe it. This *is* The Observer. Distinguish where you feel it in your body. Notice the increased heart rate and tightening of muscles. Pay attention to the energy going to your hands, how the nervous impulses and compulsions in your body instantly feel different. It just takes a few seconds to **monitor the intensity of the**

reaction on a scale of 1 to 10. One means you barely notice there is a reaction and 10 means you are experiencing an off-the-charts internal explosion. This is all internal. No behavioral response has occurred yet. The Observer is after just the facts: How would you rate the intensity of the reaction within your brain on a scale of 1 to 10?

2. Once The Observer in you has established the number, *name* **the emotion that you feel most strongly**. Because the limbic brain generates the emotion of fear, the combination of emotions you feel when you combine emotions from both the limbic and prefrontal lobes can be confusing. Most often, it is difficult to name just one emotion, because we often feel overwhelmed in the experience of the internal explosion. Naming the emotion helps you find your way through the reaction to uncover just what is really happening. Do you feel anger, frustration, hurt, rage, disappointment or some other feeling? Stay in this process of discovery until you can both identify the intensity of reaction and name the feeling. As you seek to work with this process, you might feel simultaneous conflict emotions. You might feel rage and calm at the same time. It is possible that you would concurrently feel an intensity of anger and the impulse to laugh at the silliness of that over-reaction. This strange concoction of emotion can feel odd, for sure. But, there is nothing harmed as you spend these few seconds making such determinations. Just label what you are feeling.

---

3. Now, The Observer must **ask the emotion what it wants.** This might take practice, because it is difficult at first to even comprehend the assignment. But once The Observer has found the way through the intensity of reaction to both rate the intensity and name the emotion, you likely will find that the emotion is different than what you initially experienced as the reaction. Rather than feeling intense anger, you might find that the real emotion fueling all of this anger is hurt. So it is to the hurt that The Observer asks the question, "What does the hurt (or whatever the specific emotions is) want? What would help soothe that emotion right now?"

I must digress here, because there are a few important elements to remember about the capabilities of the limbic brain. It has no ability to relate to time, so hurtful events that happened in the past easily can become a part of what is happening in the present moment. If one small part of what you just reacted to has something about it that is similar to an injustice that you experienced at, say, age 5, the rattlesnake will bring up those unresolved emotions from that time and you will experience them as part of what is occurring in the present. I know that seems strange and difficult to comprehend, but it happens frequently.

Therefore, when you ask the emotion what it wants, you may think "soothing," which does not relate to the current situation. But do it anyway. The Observer has brought it to your attention, but YOU do it. You are a grown person now, not a helpless, undefended child. You can bring wisdom and soothing to this current situation—give the emotion what it is asking for. You might find that holding your hand over your heart and being still with yourself for a few seconds is helpful. Tending to the unresolved emotions from misfortune or abuse that happened years ago and bringing love to those emotions will help the reaction you are having right now.

4. Once the emotions have settled within you, remember that all of this has happened internally. There has been no dialogue, so far, with the person who precipitated the reactive threat. It is vital that this process occur through The Observer, which you have enlisted to watch and gain facts about the reaction you are feeling. It only takes a few seconds to complete this part of the process.

5. Now you are ready to make a decision. Feeling calmer, less reactive and certainly less programmed to follow the impulses of the limbic brain, **what choice would *you* like to make at this moment?** You may not be ready yet to rely on the capability of reason, logic and bonding from your prefrontal lobes, because you understand that they are not in an optimal blend of brain chemicals to do their best cognitive work. But you at least can rely on your good judgment to do what is in the best interest of your relationship—not blast it to pieces. Remember, we cannot control our biological impulses, but we can

control our behavior. So, in using your good judgment, does it make sense to choose to:

- Firmly tell yourself, "Stop! I cannot think reasonably right now."

- Take a short break and talk about the event later when all of your brain can support better conversation.

- Go for a little walk to help the stress hormones clear out from your prefrontal lobes.

- Tell your partner or friend that there is something you would like to talk about, but you first need a few minutes to clear your mind.

- Go work out in the yard for a few minutes to get caught up on pulling weeds.

- Say a prayer or meditate for a short while.

- Breathe, smile and forget about the whole thing, because nothing really significant needs to be discussed.

- Tell yourself that you have survived these intense reactions before and they are not life-threatening and will not last long.

Most often, the first thing that will be necessary is to take a break. Even if you have decided that the reaction was unjustified, you still have the elevated levels of stress hormones with which to deal. The emotions that were accelerated when the rattlesnake quickly took over are still there. You can decide that they are an overreaction. You might decide that you would like to talk about something, but after a climate of calm has been restored. When the elevated emotions are likely still there, give yourself some time to soothe them.

Emotional Regulation

What has been described are strategies and techniques that help the regulation of emotions. This does not mean, however, that emotions are suppressed. Rather, they are felt, understood and dealt with. What it does mean is that we also understand the venomous potential that words and actions can have in our love relationships. We have matured to having the ability to recognize individual capability and responsibility in managing our biologically hard-wired reactions, and the emotions created from these. The goal is, first, observation of emotion even when great discomfort is experienced as the emotion escalates and then managing the discomfort without necessarily following the compelling impulses that are hormonally and psychologically driven.

Successful people learn this skill. They practice, so they are able to manage the direction of their lives. They realize that, otherwise, their emotional wellness is conditional, and they constantly live with the vulnerability that something in the external environment will trigger yet another undesirable outburst. Living this way is unacceptable for them.

You Have This
Capable Part in You to Work With

Please read these previous two paragraphs, and then put the book down for a few minutes. Thinking about how you might work with these ideas can feel overwhelming. You are training your body to withstand a strong biological surge and learning to manage it in a different way than you have before. It comes with appreciating the survival mechanism of the brain for the good it does, yet not allowing it to disrupt and sabotage the goals and dreams of your most important relationships.

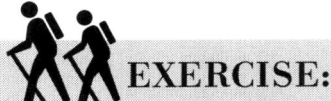 **EXERCISE:**

Recall a time when you were in the company of another person. The age of this person is insignificant. Think of a time when someone you care about was completely out of control in your presence. It could be a young toddler or a friend. You tried to remain calm. You retained stability during a time when someone else was emotionally unbridled—even raging. Your voice was steady and you were appropriately affectionate and supportive. With practice, you can do this for yourself, too. Even if you are the one who is hurt and raging, you also can be the one who brings quiet and calm.

Continue to reflect for a few minutes, and write down the specific people and even specific situations that seem to predictably 'trigger' these exaggerated responses for you. You can list a few of these in the lines provided, and it may also be useful to journal about what feelings arise within as you ponder these anticipated reactions.

1. _____

_____

2. _____

_____

3. _____

_____

Summary

I am confident that, as you read this chapter, you will shift in how you view your own possibilities as a partner. I hope that it will inspire your desire to assume greater responsibility for your own reactions through increased understanding of how your brain works. Additionally, I trust that your desire to work with those natural impulses has increased, as you now know that you are not sentenced to follow those impulses, when they would not serve the long-term best interest of your life. Perhaps you will now have greater compassion for yourself and for your spouse as you watch this survival mechanism play itself out, hopefully with decreasing frequency. The important message of this chapter is that you <u>can</u> take responsibility for how your thoughts, feelings, and impulses are expressed, even though you cannot change the fact that you are hard-wired to have those impulses. This is liberating and exciting, because it frees us to create the relationships that we deeply want and deserve. And, it allows us greater compassion towards our mates and mankind, because we better understand.

Margaret Johansen, M.S., MFT

CHAPTER 2

The Art of Listening and the Structure of Speaking

According to German-American Christian existentialist philosopher and theologian Paul Tillich, "The first duty of love is to listen." Tillich was a wise man.

More than 7,000 languages are actively spoken in today's world. This means many more than 7,000 ways to listen exist—more than any individual ever can hope to master.

Listening may be motivated by a number of agendas. Sometimes it seeks understanding with compassion and full attention. At other times, listening starts with reinforcing a preformed judgment or rejecting an idea, inflating an ego or deflating a speaker. Listening can seek to acquire knowledge, understanding or the exchange of information. The intention brought to the act of listening largely determines what will be heard.

True listening is paying attention. It is putting aside cell phones and iPads. It is turning off a television program, making full eye contact, and bringing complete attention to hearing and understanding. Listening is more than just a physical discipline. It is also an important ritual that enhances the quality of relationships.

Listening takes courage. Sometimes the one who is talking needs to feel real love and belonging, or they will be unable to reveal sensitive ideas about their imperfections or problems. You must allow yourself to be vulnerable to help support the courage it takes for them to do this. So much of the vital stuff of life lies in the vulnerability that many of us simply don't want to face. Vulnerability may access the reservoir of unworthiness that make us human, but it also exposes us to the core of human shame. So powerful is this shame that we distract, numb and avoid being intimately known in order to limit our exposure.

For this reason, it is important to bring compassion to the act of listening. Particularly when the truth is hard to verbalize, a speaker needs a receptive audience, a fundamental fact we often overlook or ignore. We only can pretend that our refusal to listen doesn't have an impact on people; it's a fantasy to expect all will end well when we neglect this basic fact. Because it won't.

The Sound of Silence

The first step toward compassionately listening is quieting your own thoughts. The mind is like a monkey—it chatters endlessly with its own agenda. In Eastern thought, this is called "monkey mind," because they find it amusing. Monkey mind is descriptive of the brain on autopilot. It attempts to distract from genuine thought by creating an avalanche of irrelevant gibberish. Often emotional frustration or negativity is at the base of this chatter. But the consistent quality is that it is ongoing, unbridled chatter. With no real benefit or even constructive conclusions, we blab away with gibberish, contributing only to stress and negativity to both our biology and psychology.

The best way to work with such a brain is to exercise your right to practice silence.

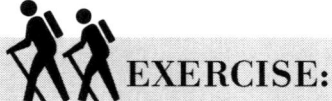

EXERCISE:

Practice creating small moments of silence while you wait at a red light. Teach yourself the discipline of non-thought. For those brief moments, clear your mind and create a vacant space. Think nothing. If words enter your mind, smile and invite them to leave. Quiet and void the chatter and become aware of just the red light.

In a culture in which distraction and busyness define the norm, this little exercise takes some practice. You may find it to be a delightful challenge, even amusing in its difficulty. You are learning to discipline the mind. Learning to cultivate quiet on demand opens up possibilities that don't exist when your mind streams chatter into every conversation you have.

You will be much more engaged in conversations when you have learned to silence the mental chatter. You can bring remarkable understanding to the most sensitive topics. When you synchronize your mental quiet with your intention to understand someone, even your body language and facial expressions become alert. Closeness in a relationship is groomed by understanding. Caring and focused attention work together in concert when we speak and listen with the intention to understand.

What Handicaps Good Listening?

We live in a unique time when the number of distractions to true listening can be habitual. Some people are so tied to their electronics—cell phones, iPads, gaming devices, television—they feel imposed upon whenever they are asked to put their distraction away and talk. Not listening can be simply the result of a bad habit.

If environmental factors were all that was involved, listening could be improved by a change in manners. However, other factors are not changed so easily. As we've seen, heightened emotions are a major cause of poor listening. Think of the all times when you felt so angry or hurt that you found it impossible to listen well. If you haven't learned to manage the intensity and target of your emotional responses, you will continue to compromise your ability to listen with compassion.

Some people were so injured by childhood traumas that they continue to view themselves as victims in need of defense. These people filter their conversations through a victim's lens. The victim mentality robs a person of his or her own internal resources of honesty, courage and ability. A self-proclaimed victim struggles to hear accurately, while focused listening is almost out of the question. This handicap is described eloquently by Wayne Muller in *Legacy of the Heart; The Spiritual Advantages of a Painful Childhood.*

Mirroring

Mirroring is a form of active listening that has been taught as a communication skill for decades. It requires that you put your ideas and responses aside and suspend your urge to speak. Mirroring means that you first listen to the thoughts, feelings and opinions of the other person. You need temporarily to constrain your thoughts and feelings, even if you disagree with what is being said. Mirroring requires that you be attentive to what is said and restrain your defensiveness, feedback and responses, until you have heard and understood the perspective of the other. You have to quiet your mind and suspend your own judgments and agenda.

You don't have to agree with or endorse what the other person says, but you do have to respect the right of the other person to say what's on his or her mind. Surely, you care enough about your relationship to make hearing what your partner has to say as important as expressing your own thoughts and ideas. In the end, you also will have the opportunity to speak and be heard. But be wise enough to know that problems cannot be solved when either of you has elevated emotions. Hear the other and, for the time being, simply listen and paraphrase.

This is not an easy skill to learn. With practice, though, it can become automatic when the situation calls for it. Mirroring is merely paraphrasing what your partner says. It allows the prefrontal cortex to retell what has been spoken without making any additions, judgments, objections, refutations or reactions. Heed the words of Joe Friday in the old TV show *Dragnet*: "Just the facts, Ma'am." Seek to learn "just the content" and add nothing.

The prefrontal cortex of the human brain seeks closeness and intimacy. It creates emotions of bonding. It is responsible for the peace, connection and feeling of satisfaction you feel when you discuss sensitive topics peacefully and reasonably. Mirroring is a skill practiced by a well-nourished Observer. You can deal reliably with difficult subjects, and you can be trusted to manage your emotions. Mirroring, as practiced by The Observer, produces greater relaxation and calm, because it sends a message to the rattlesnake brain of you and your partner that you are both safe. In safety, you can build trust, because your rattlesnake senses security, not threat.

So, how do you do mirroring? It's a fairly simple process of self-control that you can master with practice.

EXERCISE:
MIRRORING

1. At the time you notice your partner's emotions becoming elevated, postpone your own speaking and practice complete, focused listening. Your time to

---

speak will come, but let the emotional intensity subside first.

2. Don't interrupt your partner. When you do speak, you only will paraphrase what you have understood your partner to say. In doing this, use specific language, such as:

   - "What I believe you are saying right now is ..."
   - "What I get out of what you just said is ..."
   - "My understanding of what you are saying is..."
   - "What I think you want me to 'get' right now is..."
   - "What I hear you saying is ..."

3. Verify what was said to assure your partner you have understood. It is critical that you do this respectfully and not dismissively. Your partner's rattlesnake brain is hyperalert and hypersensitive. If you seem to be mocking or critical, you will sabotage the entire process. Throughout the dialogue, maintain your goodwill. If you show the tiniest edge of disrespect or sarcasm, mirroring cannot work. If your partner hears a negative judgment behind your restatement, his or her rattlesnake is likely to wake up.

4. If your partner feels that you are listening and not counterattacking, there will be no threat or perceived threat by either you or your rattlesnake brain. You can both calm down and the prefrontal parts of the brain can reassert their vitality.

Mirroring originally was developed for managing prison inmates. Prison psychologists have discovered when emotions are agitated, the very perception that people are being listened to rapidly decreases the tension and makes communication possible. It works for hardened prisoners, and it can work for you.

Brain Activity Differes for Extroverts and Introverts

Extroverts:
Individuals with the personality characteristic of being extroverts relate to people in their external world. To process their thoughts, they must dialogue out loud. "Thinking out loud" is what helps them accomplish reasoning, logic, and problem solving. Their listening audience can be another person, a family pet, or a wall. But, speaking out loud helps them facilitate neuro-transmitter connection and motion within their brain, which helps them arrive at conclusions. If they are prohibited from talking, by either the refusal to talk by another person, or if the situation itself constrains them, their process of reasoning becomes less efficient and they easily can become confused and frustrated.

An extrovert can quickly listen to contrasting new information, which may be a comment or response from their spouse, and are immediately ready to talk again. Their thought process requires that they talk to think — so they come to conclusions and even observations through dialogue. Occasionally, the extrovert will feel it all come together; it 'clicks', and they will say, "OK. This is it!" Or, "Now I have it......" This shift within the extrovert defines the moment when they are now ready to discuss something, to really share what they have concluded. In a way, it is important to respectfully listen to the preamble that comprises the thinking process of the extrovert, but it is when they have navigated the maze of neural processing through audible talk, that you might perk up and really pay attention.

Introverts:
Individuals with the personality characteristic of being introverted rely on their internal world. They listen to information from others, take it in, and bounce it around with the rest of what they know or feel. Their ability to reason and problem-solve is centered in having time alone to think, which they do reliably within themselves. They 'think and feel' through the maze of their brain, and then the come to a conclusion. This is when they might be ready to talk. Sharing with their partner what has already been completely thought through is their version of 'dialogue'.

Extroverts and Introverts
in Conversation, Together

With these two varied styles of thinking and problem solving, it is important that there is understanding about how to best work with each style of engagement with life; one internal and the other external. Since we are hard-wired to be primarily one or the other, there is not a 'right way' to be or communicate. It is merely a task of figuring out what each predominant style is, and respecting the communication necessities of that style. So, let's take a hypothetical journey together now.

Introvert communicating with an Extrovert:
The *introvert* will most likely have thought out the topic of needed discussion. Consideration will not only have been given to the actual topic, but often even how the spouse might receive the ideas and thoughts. Adjustments may already have been made on what would allow the dialogue to go well, and what might trigger emotional responses. The *introvert* has little need to share <u>how</u> conclusions were arrived at, merely giving a sort of 'report' to the spouse about what has been thought about.

As the *extrovert* listens to the topic, it requires discipline to just do a good job of listening, because all kinds of questions and reactions come to the surface. Because processing of thought requires verbally speaking, the questions and concerns just keep piling up in their mind, throughout the task of listening. The *extrovert* might do well to just have pencil in hand and make a list of these reactions; otherwise frustration can be overwhelming.

When it becomes the *extrovert's* turn to respond to the

content of what the *introvert* has said, they will want to do it immediately. The longer they must wait with thoughts, reactions and ideas internally in their head, the more confused or frustrated they become. Their thoughts will not be cohesive and thought through. The listener must understand that the *extrovert* 'thinks out loud', so the meandering and even conflicting thought that is spoken at first is listened to, but not taken as final conclusion. The *introvert* must remember that they do this too — it just is done internally, not verbally. The *extrovert* might occasionally say something like, "Well, I didn't mean what I said earlier, this is what I really mean." And, it's true!

As the *introvert* listens to the *extrovert*, the *introvert* will take in the information. Most often, the *introvert* will want to take a few minutes, then, to consider what has been said. Internally bouncing the new information around between their mind and their feelings, they will once again come up with a 'summary' to verbally present.

The *extrovert* will do well to understand that, if they want to learn about the process of thought that guided the *introvert* arrived at conclusions, they need to ask about it. This is because the *introvert* feels complete in just internally considering their own thought and feeling. They really have no compelling need to share how they arrived at a new consideration or conclusion. But, the *extrovert* can feel deprived of vital information if this is not shared — so the *extrovert* must ask if it is important.

Consider that the *extrovert* has a difficult time 'waiting' as the *introvert* takes thinking time. Since the *extrovert* has great difficulty processing information or coming to any conclusion without verbally speaking out loud, having unresolved information in their brain with no way to process it is difficult. So, it is incumbent upon the *introvert* to return to dialogue as soon as possible. There is no hurry, really, on the part of the *introvert*, because their content will be self-resolved as they consider the next step of conversation. But, in the meanwhile, the *extrovert* might be going nuts!

Working back and forth, in segments of conversation, is a structure that works well for couples that have the *extrovert* and *introvert* dynamic between them. If each respects the inherent style of the other — communication can progress along seamlessly. If these two styles engage competitively with each other, the *introvert* will likely explode at some time, because the *extrovert* demands dialogue. Frustration heightens within the *introvert*, as there is no respect given for their need to be alone and think.

Conversely, if the *extrovert* is not given opportunity to speak, frustration will be heightened within the *extrovert*. Additionally, respect must be given for the external component of the *extrovert's* thinking style, and allowance made for what feels inconsistent and even conflicted in their thinking. The *introvert* must listen for the <u>shift</u> that signals the *extrovert's* arrival at clarity and conclusion.

How Couples Successfully
Can "Get Through" A Conversation

The Observer, practicing mirroring, can de-escalate the compulsions of the rattlesnake brain. The next task is to shift from de-escalation to resolution. The first order of business is to progress into dialogue.

After you have managed reactions by using The Observer process and perhaps taken a short break, you are now ready to talk. While you are taking your break, write down the specific things you need to talk about. You do this to focus the dialogue and prevent the discussion from shifting. If the discussion turns into a free-for-all, it becomes much more difficult to stay on task and employ the problem-solving abilities of the prefrontal brain to lead to resolution. The rattlesnake begins to perceive a threat whenever you allow the discussion to lose direction.

Talk to your partner in about 30 second capsules. Keep these capsules short, so accurate reflection (mirroring) can occur. When either of you are speaking, interruption by the other is not allowed. Some couples even pass a rod or something to hold physically as a reminder of who has the floor.

Each time you have completed your 30-second capsule of communication; your partner then paraphrases back what he or she has heard. This should not be a parroting of your exact words. Rather, your partner should capture the essence of what you just said to show that he or she really understood your meaning.

If your partner misunderstands, leaves anything out or makes any errors, immediately correct the misunderstandings, fill in omissions and straighten out any misunderstandings. This is not a test or a contest. Your goal is understanding, not redemption.

Each time the paraphrase process is completed and accurate, it is your turn again. Take another 30 seconds to present another capsule. Continue in this fashion until you have communicated what you desire to say and feel completely satisfied that you have been listened to and understood. Don't consider the situation resolved at this point, because only one of you has had an opportunity to speak. But be calm and know you have been heard and understood.

Now trade turns. You have had your time in the spotlight, now it is your partner's turn to be the center of attention. The same rules apply to you. Don't interrupt, and hear what your partner has to say with as much respect as you expected from them.

This attempt to deeply listen to your mate as you postpone your own response can create some discomfort. It is not unusual to suppose 'discomfort' means something is *wrong*. We often try to counter this discomfort by becoming agitated, elevated in our tone of voice and emotions, or desire to leave the conversation. Isn't it interesting that these shifts mirror the same survival mechanisms employed by the limbic brain: fight, flight, and freeze. Interesting, because trying to maintain that which is familiar brings a feeling of safety and security. Conversely, moving beyond that which is familiar is perceived by the brain as a potential threat. So, what you are feeling *does* provoke the attention of the rattlesnake brain. It is important to understand that this is normal, so you can soothe your own discomfort, reassure those feelings that all is well, and tell that part of your own brain that you are *intentionally* moving beyond your comfort zone in an effort to enhance long-term love! Please just remind yourself that 'discomfort' is not 'wrong' or 'bad'. It is just unfamiliar.

When you really listen to each other, you'll find few differences that cannot find a common platform of compromise. We usually muddle the listening and understanding, because we abort the process of a 'meeting of the minds' before dialogue can get off the ground. Our rattlesnake brain does a great job of making judgments and biting. The mere act of progressing through dialogue to empathetic acceptance is enormous progress.

Expanding the mechanics of problem solving, when just understanding the position of the other person does not bring resolution, you can use a formal problem-analysis process. Below is a suggestion for a template that may be of use in trying to bring actual resolution to the task of problem solving. There are many benefits to using such a template. It helps keep the focus of problems or differences on a sheet of paper, rather than transferring unresolved problems into personal issues or perceived flaws of the other person. It helps to keep the dialogue focused on the matter at hand. A template helps the couple think 'outside the box', reaching for possible solutions that might not otherwise occur to them. It helps break a problem down into component parts, and allows steps towards a resolution to be a sufficient conclusion, rather than needing a fully-resolved solution before the couple can settle into a course of action. If you can define a few steps that you are willing to start out with, and set a date a few weeks in the future at which time the proposal will be mutually reviewed, then you can continue to work with the problem as a process. Sometimes, needing a final 'solution' as a prerequisite for taking any steps towards problem-solving actually acts as a barrier that discourages doing any thing at all.

In the last section of this template, we are creating a 'pilot program'. I well know a gentleman who primarily uses his airplane to travel within the United States. He once explained to me that, when flying, the plane is always 'off course'. A pilot necessarily corrects the plane to account for wind, elevation, temperature, storm fronts and other turbulence. The important information to know is your final destination. Everything else is on constant course correction. I like to think of the last section of this template as a pilot program, meaning it defines attempts at course-corrections. It is tentative, perhaps, maybe in its nature. But, it is a course you agree upon as something to try for a period of time. Doing this takes pressure off of the outcome.

If I am going to 'try' to see if I like a dish cooked with jalapeno peppers, it's just a taste. If I like them, great. If I love it, I'll keep eating them. If I really don't like them, no big deal — it was just a taste. There is no one at fault if I didn't like them — I just discovered something new. So, try to think of this last section as discovery, not a final solution.

EXERCISE:
PROBLEM-SOLVING MATRIX

Goal/Problem

_____

_____

_____

_____

_____

_____

What does 100 percent look like when this problem has been solved?

_____

_____

_____

_____

What are we already doing that works toward 100 percent resolution?

1. _____

2. _____

3. _____

4. _____

What is currently in the way of creating or is sabotaging 100 percent resolution?

1. _____

2. _____

3. _____

4. _____

What can we experiment with, change or start doing that will contribute to achievement of 100 percent resolution? This is just a 'pilot program', to be tried for a set period of time. Results will be evaluated within _____ weeks.

1. _____

2. _____

3. _____

4. _____

Date_____

Lesson:

You have now expanded your normal comfort zone, and have found that when you stay calm and rational even through difficult or sensitive conversations, you experience a greater sense of trust and safety. You also become more confident that you and your partner share respect for each other's thoughts and feelings.

If It Is Urgently Needed, Exercise Your Rights!!!

- You may request a five-minute monologue at any time it is needed. Agree with your partner on a signal or sequence of words that announces this request. It can be as simple as, "I need five minutes." Set the timer. You now have the floor without interruption of any kind, not even paraphrasing. When the five minutes have been spent, your spouse may then take an uninterrupted five-minute turn, if desired. This can be mobilized at any time—but in five minutes, your time is done.

- You also can take a one-hour break, if you assess that conversation has gone beyond what you can manage. You may go for a drive, take a walk, read, draw or engage in some other activity that is a break for you. At the end of the hour, it is important that you keep your commitment to return and make every effort to resume the conversation. The intention is not to avoid dialogue but to contribute to its success by managing your own emotional state.

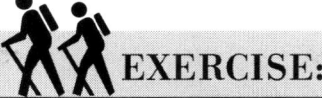 **EXERCISE:**

Reverberation

Reverberation, or echoing, is merely the process of getting in the habit of repeating exactly what was said to you. It is just for short little tasks. Here are some examples:

- Request: Honey, will you please pick up Harley from school at 3 o'clock.

  Response: OK, I just heard that you would like me to pick up Harley from school at 3 o'clock, is that right?

- Request: Can you please take the car to get the oil changed? Oh, and have them check the air filter while you're there?

  Response: OK, You're asking if I can take the car to get the oil changed and the air filter checked, right? Does that need to be done today or sometime this week?

- Request: Do you mind taking the clothes out of the washer and putting them in the dryer as soon as you arrive home this afternoon?

  Response: Am I hearing that you would like me to take the clothes from the washer and put them in the dryer as soon as I get home today?

These are such simple reverberations — just to be sure that you are on 'the same page'. It helps immensely to clarify conversation and, especially requests. The number of 'blame game' arguments that have occurred in the past will naturally decrease. Simple and, perhaps sometimes annoying. But, compared to the arguments that ensue because someone says a request was never made, or at least never heard, it is yet another tip that brings great benefit!

Relieving The Tension of Conflict

Most of the time, our conversations go wrong, because we are too impatient to listen to the other person. We pay half-attention when they are talking. Mirroring is the antidote. It's not practical to apply mirroring every moment of every day. But when you notice that your partner's emotions are beginning to escalate, it is time to pause. Understand that you are speaking with someone who has switched into the limbic brain and recognize that conversation as usual will not be productive.

A good rule to follow is not to participate in dialogue whenever you or your partner is under the control of the rattlesnake. Listening and diffusing emotions by paraphrasing and mirroring is always appropriate whenever intense emotions surface. But don't offer any responses, ideas, suggestions — and certainly not blame or projections — until both of you have restored calm. If you deem it beneficial, you can suggest taking a short break by using one of the following statements:

- "That's a good point. I'll think about this and get right back to you."

- "I can see you feel strongly about that. Let me mull it over and see how I feel about it. We'll talk in just a little while."

- "What an interesting perspective. I need some time to consider what you have said and then we can talk."

In any case, the intention is to build time into the structure of the discussion, thus allowing time for stress hormones to dissipate out of the brain which restores a condition of calm. You are not agreeing or responding, just affirming that you have heard the content of what your partners has said, and that you will give consideration to these points and will return and talk. In doing this, you are also delaying conversation intentionally, just giving time for the body to restore normal calm.

This Does NOT Endorse Abuse!

Now it's time to address the circumstance of relationship abuse. Effective communication comes from internal strength, love and generosity. Abusive behaviors have no part in any relationship. Our brain's hardwiring predisposes us to favor the rattlesnake whenever our safety feels threatened. When you understand what that means, you can give space to your partner when their rattlesnake comes to the surface and you can expect, in turn, that your partner will be generous and forgiving when your rattlesnake is awakened.

Abuse happens when this does not occur. Unrestrained, aggressive confrontation without apology for personal words and actions is abusive. The abuser blames the partner for provoking the abuse and sets out to punish and demean with poisonous put-downs intended to make the receiver feel inadequate or wrong. Abuse often is motivated by a desire to be right or in control. Communication becomes buried under a thirst for social approval and validation so amplified that it takes on an obsessive significance and obliterates an honest appraisal of Self.

How long you should continue investing in a relationship when your partner refuses to accept responsibility for his or her role in it is an intimate and personal decision. Accommodating another's abuse is never part of your personal growth, however. Individuals who have the strength, determination and character necessary to learn these mirroring strategies also have the right to make long-term decisions regarding their own best interest.

Ending a Conversation
When It Becomes Too Critical

Mirroring and reflecting is not the same thing as allowing your spouse to dominate your life or get away with chronic criticism. If your partner uses dialogue as an exercise in domination, or if the dialogue has deteriorated into a barrage of criticism, it is appropriate to end the conversation by saying something such as, "It feels like this is no longer a constructive expression of something to be solved or even discussed; it feels like a blasting of criticism. I am not going to engage in this but hope we can try again another time." Or, "You are giving me a long list of complaints, and I only can reasonably work with a few at a time. We either need to focus on just a few or we'll need to continue this conversation another time."

Summary

Couples who practice this adult form of understanding and communication experience mutual healing and growth. They take responsibility for comprehending the nature of their own human brain and emotions. Not only do they manage their own neurological compulsions and impulses, they also develop greater kindness toward and understanding of their partner. They *want* to enhance their intimacy, and that desire, more than anything else, makes success possible. Listening with respect is one of the highest forms of honoring another person. We each *want* to be heard and understood. We desire that our voice can honestly communicate. I believe that most people do not desire to hurt another, but just want to feel love for another and be loved. Listening well is one of the foundational principles that helps this to occur.

CHAPTER 3

The Joy And Benefit Of Play

I grew up in the foothills of the Angeles National Forest, a rural part of Southern California where people had property and kept horses, peacocks and other animals not typically allowed by city zoning. After our chores were done on Saturday morning, the seven children in my family often would ride off on our bikes to a flood control dam a few miles away, where reeds and cattails grew, and frogs, wild rabbits and other small animals were plentiful. My mother and father were never concerned about where we were. By the end of Saturday, after all the yard work, housecleaning, and long bike rides and other play activities, we were pretty worn out and satisfied.

We had plenty of bonding moments on those Saturday afternoons. We strategized to catch an especially large frog. We shared the joy of discovering dragonflies and hummingbirds. We hid in the tall grasses and spied on folks having picnics near the water. We delighted at catching a glimpse of a fox or coyote. Then we'd ride home and tell everyone else about our adventures with a sparkle in our eyes and laughter in our voices.

These memories are filled with the attributes of play—connection, engagement, group camaraderie and bonding, chaos and edginess, creativity and imagination, figuring things out and planning, physical exertion, group activities, sharing, problem solving, exhaustion, freedom and abandonment, control of our own schedules, unexpected surprises and, most of all, pleasure and enjoyment.

In our over-scheduled adult lives, play too often takes a backseat. Even children do not play as much as they once did. Our children increasingly have moved their leisure time indoors. Children in this country spend an average of four hours every day in front of the television and 13.2 hours each week playing video games. This is not bad, per se, but it does indicate just how the content of play has become less active and involved.

In America, adults put in at least eight hours a day at work and an additional hour or so for lunch. They then return home, where many of them spend additional hours on such family tasks as preparing meals, cleaning up the kitchen, spending time with their children, unwinding and relaxing, catching up on personal emails or the news, and tending to their own hygiene. It could be worse; it is typical in the oriental culture for a workday to extend to 16 hours per day, with only a few days off per year. Recreation in its original sense is neglected in favor of more pressing obligations.

The more we focus on adult tasks, the less attention we pay to play. We choose to pay attention to the responsibilities of career, education, marriage and family, home and cars, and perhaps community involvement, while we give little time to recreation. Each of these "responsible" activities brings unique stresses and demands we never had to deal with when we were younger. We still may set aside some time for play, but we wrestle that time away from seemingly more important endeavors.

An Internet search on the subject of adult play shows how little attention is paid to adult play activities. Search Google for "active adult play" and you'll get a long list of ways adults can help children engage in active play but only a handful of articles about adult play. Even more telling, the bible of play, *The Praeger Handbook of Play Across the Life Cycle: Fun from Infancy to Old Age* by Luciano L'Abate, tells us that most middle-age adults equate "play" with exercise, which they consider an obligation, not a recreation. The simple fact is, adults just don't play.

That's not to say that exercise is not important, especially as we age. One sign of aging is too often a flagging motivation to exercise. Most people realize that they will be weaker and less energetic if they don't stay in shape. They'll have less stamina and endurance for work and leisure. Most people who do exercise take an occasional day off, but it costs them in the long run if they make taking time off a habit. So they make an intellectual choice to exercise. But often it's exercise for the sake of exercise, not for the intrinsic rewards of exercise itself.

Reasons why couples do not play

People are very creative in finding reasons not to play. They "can't" play because:

- They have a new child.
- They've lost a job or changed their employment.
- They are working on developing new work relationships.
- They are committed to building their business.
- They have problems with their children or marriage
- They're dealing with a death of a family member or close friend.
- Their children are leaving home.
- They have to get ready for a family wedding.

- They've had an accident or injury.

- They're suffering from a prolonged illness.

- They're experiencing financial loss or hardship.

- They've decided to return to school.

- They're moving.

- They're getting divorced.

- They have to change the furnace filters.

In reality, why should these reasons become more compelling than play? Part of the problem is that people do not acknowledge or recognize the full benefits that play offers. Playing is often considered frivolous or something to enjoy if there is time after the "important" things have been taken care of. Playing is a "luxury" that often involves too much effort.

Powerful emotions like anger, frustration, despair and resentment may interfere with our desires to play. A few people cannot even anticipate the pleasure of play, because they've experienced a trauma or other difficulty. If we feel misunderstood or not cared about, we may not feel like playing. The reality is, though, that the less we play, the less we feel affection and connection and the less we feel positive about our partner, which leads to more resentment. Couples will do well to focus on ingredients that contribute positively to their relationship. Play is one of those ingredients. Few life events warrant denying pleasure and enjoyment.

HOW YOUR BRAIN AND
LIFE BENEFIT FROM PLAY

Play Connects Us to Others

Shared play is one of the most effective ways to keep relationships vital and exciting. Sharing laughter and play adds resilience, joy and vitality to our lives. Play is the only activity that produces the feel-good hormones that we experience with physical exercise and the bonding hormones that strengthen our relationships. The hormone oxytocin is released during play, in addition to the feel-good chemicals serotonin, dopamine and endorphins.

Four of my grandchildren and I went rock climbing in the volcanic spew near St. George, Utah. The older grandchildren, ages 6 and 11, bolted ahead and began climbing some fairly high rock walls, leaving the dejected 4-year-old Zoei and me behind to watch from the trail. I suggested that we find a wall that was our size and climb it, just the two of us. So off we went to find a special, kid-size obstacle that would be our wall.

Our first challenge was about 12 feet high. We cautiously made our way to the top and back down. With that success, we were ready for more. We found a second wall about 20 feet tall. Filled with the confidence of endorphins, Zoei climbed to the top of this one and then yet another one that was 10 feet higher.

When Zoei returned to the trail, the others were just coming around the corner. She threw her body into an exuberant warrior pose and with all the gusto and volume she could muster, shouted out, "I'm A-SE-SOME!" (feel-good chemicals) And then, with the same gusto, she threw her arms around my legs and shouted with the same intensity, "You're the best grandma ever!" (bonding hormones)

Play Helps Build Trust and Enables Us To Try New Things

When we engage in play, we push edges. Whether this is because of the competition or the opportunities for expansion, play is more than fun. It arouses our curiosity and introduces the novelty of challenge. During play, we are more willing to risk and experiment through trial and error. Think about the first time you tried snow skiing or waterskiing; you probably fell many times. It was a natural part of the learning process. But you got up and tried again. In the experience of play, you trusted, got up and tried once more. And if someone with more experience was nearby to teach you, you experienced a new relationship, too.

Play Heals Emotional Wounds

It is impossible for a couple to be in a marriage and not occasionally hurt each other. These wounds require forgiveness; and still the memory of hurt resurfaces from time to time. Play nourishes hearts. It teaches us that life can be enjoyable again, that residual emotions don't need to dominate every moment of our days. Even if the pain is recent and raw, play allows us to connect to something larger than our problems.

The search for belonging—within yourself, within a marriage, within a family, within the global world—is one of the most enduring of urges. It is also confusing, because belonging has as much to do with the strength and health of the individual as it does with the relationship. Play facilitates both. Play helps us experience ourselves as individuals, solid and complete within our own bodies and minds. Play also transcends the individual and reminds us that we are a part of a couple or team. In the dynamic of playing as a couple, we bond in a way that connects us more deeply with each other. Giving play priority in your relationship is a powerful way to heal resentment and diminish the sting of former transgressions.

Play Helps You Function Under Stress

Stress floods our system with hormones that serve a single purpose—survival. Under normal circumstances, these chemicals, which include such hormones as cortisol and norepinephrine, do not run around in our bodies. That's fortunate. Cortisol affects the metabolic system and, if overproduced, contributes to exhaustion and autoimmune problems. Norepinephrine contributes to attention-deficit/hyperactivity disorder, depression and hypertension.

Play counteracts these stress hormones. During play, the body produces endorphins, serotonin and dopamine. These are well-established as feel-good chemicals in the brain. Even 20 minutes after playing, <u>positron emission tomography</u> scans, 3-D color images of the functional processes within the human body of brain activity, show that all areas of the brain are lit up completely. Stress hormones are absent, the brain swims in feel-good chemicals hormones, and the brain areas associated with cognition, creativity, problem solving and bonding are active.

Play stimulates the manufacture of feel-good chemicals at the same time it extinguishes stress hormones. By itself, play can have enormous benefits to a marriage. Surround any problem with laughter, a sense of humor, an array of feel-good chemicals, and you have a better platform from which to confront any problems.

Play Helps Relieve Depression

The opposite of play is not work—it is depression. The same PET scan that shows a playful brain as a fully engaged brain shows a depressed brain as deficient in humor, pleasure and reward; a brain that is disconnected and suffering from an imbalance between the frontal thinking lobe and the brain's reward centers.

Research at Yale University showed that a single genetic switch, the transcription factor, is required for brain synapses to connect with one another. When these connections aren't made, like during depression, brain mass actually can be lost. This could be disheartening news if it were not for the brain's neuroplasticity that it retains throughout a lifetime. This neuroplasticity enables the brain to heal, remold and correct its function without intervention.

Play helps defend against the depression-related atrophy of the brain. It actually can reverse some of the most common symptoms of depression, including sadness and unhappiness; irritability and frustration; reduced libido; slowed thinking; indecisiveness, distractibility and decreased concentration; as well as fatigue and loss of energy.

Active play jump-starts neuroplasticity and counters these symptoms by reconstructing areas of the brain that may be overtaxed by stress, depression or other causes. Just 10 minutes spent in the backyard with a family pet completely can change a foul mood. Repeated short-term interventions will, with time, help you regain cheerfulness and hope in your life.

In *The Gift of Play: Why Adult Women Stop Playing and How To Start Again*, Barbara Brannen describes the connection between play and the happiest times of her life. She grew up playing outdoors, hiking and spending time in the woods near her childhood home. When she later married a man who loved indoor activities, she found that something was missing. Only when she reconnected with the outdoor play that enlivened her heart did she regain the sense of wonder and contentment in her life. Once she discovered this, she realized she could enjoy playing in her husband's indoor world, too. Making time for the fulfillment of her own play needs, she began to experience a true sense of playfulness in all aspects of her life.

Play Provides Relief
from Loneliness and Isolation

Play enlivens each of us as individuals. Laughter is a social sign and universal language. Squealing and laughter can make visceral and obvious bonds among strangers who don't speak the same language.

Even when you are alone, you can experience the connections and delights of play. This is heart play, the kind of play you knew as a child that brought you to a sense of oneness with your surroundings. This individual activity fills and brings balance into the space that you may have experienced as loneliness. It brings about a sense of belonging and comfort, whether you are alone or surrounded by friends.

Laughter itself is a form of shared empathy and connection. As we play, we laugh together, enhancing the bonding and enjoyment we experience as part of a group. Hearing someone else laugh amplifies the joy of an experience. A common response to hearing another person laugh is to join in the laughter.

At the age of 64, Martha has learned that rigorous play she fully engages in can be fun and even life-saving. She still believes that she can outrun her grandchildren. She may not succeed every time they play but that's no problem. When she has spent 30 minutes laughing and racing as fast as she can, she feels deeply satisfied. She bonds with the kids as they walk with their arms around each other back to the house. Although she then is tired and ready for a good book or a rest on the couch, she is satisfied in a very special way. That's how it works—and they all love it.

Even in couples, an individual still sometimes can feel isolated. A legal contract and shared living space mean little if one doesn't feel enough intimacy in the relationship. Often overlooked, shared play is a powerful way of keeping a relationship resilient, vital and exciting.

Solitary Play

As previously mentioned, play also can be a singles' activity. A person can play alone and still connect with and delight in being alive. He or she can engage fully in the experience of the moment and intensify the feeling of vitality. After rigorous solitary play, a person feels revitalized, joyful and alive. All of the benefits of enhanced brain chemistry and function are available when we play alone or with a friend.

Margaret Johansen, M.S., MFT

Who says you can't play if you're alone? I live in a community for people 55 years of age and older with a number of other single people. That doesn't stop me from having fun. It offers many clubs from which I can choose. I go to the gym and participate in dance and even hip-hop classes. I can join a performing arts club or any of the groups who hike and travel together. I can play bridge, hearts and pinochle. I can enjoy laughter and humor and fun, whether I do it alone or with someone.

Solitary play definitely has its place. True solitary play is something you do with no one but yourself, such as hiking alone, planning an excursion for just you or having an adventure by yourself. One of my clients travels to Nepal and does humanitarian work with Nepalese girls. The purpose feeds her soul as much as the play, because it enriches her life and enables her to help others. Her involvement goes far beyond play. It fulfills her emotional needs and gives her an ongoing sense of purpose.

RESOURCES AND IDEAS FOR PLAY

The following is a list of alternatives for adult play. After reading the list, you may find a few new ways for you and your partner to add more play to your lives. Add ideas of your own and make play a part of your routine. It will enrich both your life and marriage.

Cultural Activities

- Find an interesting museum
- Attend a comedy performance or lounge act
- Go to a professional or community theater production
- Attend a local dance
- Visit an art gallery
- Read a book together
- Take a class
- Be a tourist in your own city
- Attend a lecture at a local university
- Attend an ethnic day and learn about a different culture
- Make friends with neighbors from a different cultural background and invite them for an afternoon gathering

Outdoor Recreation

- Go to a park, arboretum, botanical garden, aquarium or zoo
- Play flag tag or Frisbee golf
- Roll down a grassy hill
- Go to the beach
- Build a sand castle or other structure

Margaret Johansen, M.S., MFT

- Fly a kite
- Jump in the ocean, even if it is cold
- Play badminton
- Take a drive through the mountains
- Use binoculars to spot things you've never seen before
- Look for wildcats and mountain goats
- Have an outdoor picnic or barbecue
- Go skiing, snowboarding, sledding or snow tubing
- Have relay races
- Try Zumba or water Zumba
- Enter a competitive race or other athletic event
- Try driving off-road vehicles
- Go waterskiing
- Use a stand-up paddleboard
- Go white-water rafting
- Climb a tree
- Tube down a river
- Play beanbag toss
- Rent a paddleboat
- Go bird-watching
- Snorkel or scuba dive
- Go surfing or bodyboarding

- Play miniature golf

- Take a water aerobics class

- Canoe or kayak on a lake or river

- Take a sailboat out for an afternoon

- Go hiking and camping

- Ride a horse

- Draw with chalk on the sidewalk

- Ride a bike

- Play with anything that stays afloat in a tub

- Go to an airport and watch plans arrive and take off

- Take a city bus and people-watch
  or take in a matinee

- Enjoy a hot air balloon ride

- Have a tug-of-war with teams of friends

- Play tennis, paddleball or pickleball

- Walk the dog

- Ice or Roller skate

- Pretend you are in a fencing match

- Play fling ball or fling sock

- Play golf

- Go rock climbing

- Rent a Jet Ski

Dates and Events

- Discuss the larger questions of life
- Plan a fantasy vacation together
- Play laser tag
- Check out the local bookstore
- Take a short road trip
- Act out a scripted murder mystery
- Perform and film a movie just for fun
- Meditate together
- Practice yoga or exercise together
- Eat a leisurely dinner
- Cook dinner together
- Have a Hacky Sack competition
- Blow bubbles
- Play bingo
- Bat balloons back and forth
- Juggle
- Enjoy a fire in the fireplace together
- Build an outdoor fire in a pit
- Host a small dinner party
- Join a performing arts or improv group
- Target shoot

- Go to a sporting event
- Go bowling
- Create a photo album together and tell stories about the pictures
- Visit a restaurant you don't usually go to
- Take a dance class
- Jump on a trampoline
- Go to a bounce house
- Participate in karaoke
- Engage in a community or political function
- Hold a rock 'n' roll party
- Play with young children and do whatever they want to do
- Play pingpong
- Play board games
- Play croquet or bocce ball
- Draw, paint or do a craft
- Shoot pool
- Listen to or play music
- Make a snowman or have a snowball fight
- Have a water-gun fight
- Have a pillow fight

Margaret Johansen, M.S., MFT

Play That Creates Connection

- Make fun of yourself in front of your partner
- Make up a silly song
- Talk about your day
- Pay compliments
- Read joke books together
- Tell amusing and engaging stories
- Create haikus or limericks together
- Listen to a comedy CD
- Give your partner a gag gift
- Watch a movie or show together
- Give flowers
- Send a Thank You note
- Make a favorite dish
- Do a service for another
- Go to a bed-and-breakfast or a hotel for a night or weekend
- Give each other a massage or go for a couples massage
- Wash each other's hair
- Serve your partner breakfast in bed
- Pamper your partner for a day by doing all of the household chores

- Take a bubble bath or a shower together
- Sing to each other
- Watch a sunrise or sunset together
- Dress up and go out for the evening
- Create a sensual mood in your bedroom or another room
- Trace your sweetheart's face with a soft feather

Margaret Johansen, M.S., MFT

CHAPTER 4

The Art of Merging 'I' and 'We'

Since her childhood, my daughter Trina always has loved horses. Riding is her therapy and release, allowing her to work out the difficulties of her life on horseback. It's no wonder horses remain at the core of her being. Today Trina trains these majestic, strong-willed and powerful animals. Horses are capable of being very independent and stubborn; Trina lets them be a horse and follow their own nature. She places old tires in the arena, for example, and leads the horses by a tether through the desired pattern. She gradually extends the tether, so that they no longer follow her but complete the turns and footwork on their own, responding only to the length of the tether and Trina's vocal commands. Trina has learned that horses are happiest and easier to work with when they have parameters and directives. If they were allowed to be in control, riders would be in constant danger. Not only is it safer for riders to have a well-trained horse, but also both horse and rider are more contented.

In a way, children are like horses. Some run out of control, creating such chaos that they rule the house. Lacking internal direction, they are constantly at the mercy of external environments without the ability to guide their own lives. They are rewarded in the moment with a sense of power and the ability to exact immediate compliance from their parents, but they don't experience happiness.

The long-term consequences are destructive. Youth is when children grow and push boundaries, fall, make mistakes and get up and try again. It is the necessary pattern of life. Toddlers have to stumble and fall in order to balance their gait and walk. The child's brain must learn how to calculate the limits of safety and danger, to discover the boundaries of security. If children did not experiment with the external environment and, for example, break a few things, they could not learn the difference between glass, plastic and wood. Telling them that something is hazardous is not enough. Sometimes, they have to learn firsthand.

The task of childhood is to reconcile the sense of self and the external world. It is to explore understanding and feelings about race, religion, physical appearance, skills and abilities, gender orientation, ideologies, country and heritage, rules and ethics, respect for authority, education and eventually careers. It is to find a signature identification and integrity in the center of all of this—a place that fits and a definition of Me. Yet, in order to discover "me," a child must first be able to differentiate "me" from "not me." Children push, throw tantrums and run away, all in an effort to identify power and authority and the parameters that define the self.

Even parents with the best intentions sometimes abdicate their responsibilities in the face of a child's temper tantrum, giving in to the child's bad behavior instead of enforcing boundaries. This is equivalent to abandoning the good intention of teaching proper behavior and boundaries in an attempt to soothe our own anxiety about the situation, and it reinforces the message the child wants to hear: "No matter how I behave, I get what I want." It is also dangerous. Children need parameters and boundaries. Failing to enforce boundaries with a child creates chaos similar to a horse being given complete control over itself and the rider. If children learn that they will be rewarded without having to exercise self-regulation, they will never take responsibility for their own happiness; never find an ethical, social compass; and never evolve beyond a narcissistic self.

This ongoing act of self-definition doesn't end with childhood, however. It continues through much of our lives. We continually are learning about ourselves, so we are always in a state of change. If we were fortunate to be raised by parents who exercised both conditions and unconditional love, we learned the lifetime lessons that we are loved no matter what, but we also are held accountable for what we do and should do. Growing up isn't just a free ride.

Has overly permissive parenting and a culture of entitlement interfered with the process of self-definition? Are adults entering marriages still pushing and competing for a place for the unrestrained self to exist? If so, is it because we have neglected to develop the maturity upon which marriage depends?

Part of this maturity is the capacity to merge. The ability to merge is part of the ego formation that is best completed during childhood. In the normal course of growing up, we develop our signature personality. We learn to distinguish between our personal power and our power in relationships. We give shape to our spirituality or religion, career identity and gender identity. We come to an acceptance of our race and cultural history. We develop a relationship with ourselves and learn how to relate to other people. We distinguish the line between appropriate and inappropriate expression of our ego. To the extent that we successfully do develop in all of these ways, we become able to practice the fundamental skills of mature behavior including the following.

Deeply Listen with Focused Attention to Understand

Listening well is so important that it is worth revisiting. Few couples actually do it well. Often, spouses listen while silently disagreeing with their partner, thinking of their rebuttals or judging the content of what they are hearing. What they are *not* doing is focused listening.

Ed is a young doctor and Judy is his wife. While they haven't been married long, their marriage has been punctuated by long periods of separation as they each pursued graduate degrees at universities in different cities. Their marriage still suffers unresolved emotional scarring from Ed's short-term affair several years ago, and their conversations are loaded with defensive and insensitive comments. Ed regrets the affair and is resolved to not repeat the mistake.

Whenever Judy expresses an opinion about a current problem, Ed reacts as if she is once again referring to his past error. Ed then dismisses Judy's comments and feelings, because he feels attacked. He does this by quickly interrupting her and curtly demands, "We don't need to go there again." This abruptness discounts the significance of any problem needing to be addressed in the present and acts to bring that situation from a few years ago into every current dialogue. Ed unintentionally re-victimizes both of them and prolongs the process of much-needed healing.

For Ed and Judy, healing their relationship begins with listening to each other, taking turns and opening their hearts to understanding. At home, if Ed senses that Judy needs to have feelings affirmed, he could reach out a hand and touch her arm to reassure her that he desires to focus on what she is feeling in this very moment. Both have to realize that the past can be learned from but not changed. Listening is the first step in leaving the past behind and living in the present.

Listening attentively is effectual, but it is only one ingredient in the recipe. Asking your spouse about underlying fears, insecurities and hurts, and hearing the replies without defensiveness is necessary, too. It always may not lead to resolution, which may take further critical thinking and problem solving. But it does lead to understanding, and that's a necessary first step.

Engage in Critical Thinking Without Hidden Agenda

Most Americans were taught the basics of critical thinking either in high school or college. How well we've retained that information and can use what we learned is a different story! Critical thinking is actually a complex set of skills that have been defined as:

- Disciplined thinking that is clear, rational, open-minded and informed by evidence
- Purposeful, self-regulatory judgment that results in interpretation, analysis, evaluation and inference
- The intentional application of rational, higher-order thinking skills, such as analysis, synthesis, problem recognition and problem solving, inference, and evaluation

In summary, critical thinking involves:

- Purposeful self-regulation
- Careful gathering of information through analysis, observation, experience, reflection and reasoning

- Applying higher-order thinking skills
- Asking questions to obtain contextual considerations and accurate understanding
- Subordinating emotional reactions that affect impartiality
- Rejecting oversimplification
- Acknowledging that interpretations other than one's own are valid

Critical thinking is not work for sissies! It requires that you notice your own thoughts and biases. It is driven by a willingness to question both yourself and others to ensure the most rational understanding possible.

Critical thinking cannot exist where hidden agendas exist. Distorting critical thinking with an intention or manipulation is disingenuous. Critical thinking requires innocence and an intention to understand and solve the problem. It requires that we are not using a dialogue to be crafty and cunning to get our own way. True problem solving is a process that includes both empathy and negotiation. The problem is not that one person sees things the wrong way. Problem solving involves a genuine effort to find common ground with love and respect. No one starts by being right, and the objective is not to end by winning. Critical thinking is an opportunity for both parties to give priority to the relationship, to find a way to respect the *me* and the *other* without neglecting the *us*.

Negotiate Without Accusing

Why is it often difficult to negotiate even the simplest subjects? Emotional defenses flare as one person accuses the other of not giving proper consideration to feelings or needs. Simple decency suffers as each person turns the other into an object of frustration and feels equity and fairness is being thrown out the window. Somehow, the negotiation has turned into a dart-throwing competition, with parties keeping score of who wins and loses.

Fortunately, most often negotiations don't get stuck in this rut. As long as both people maintain focus on solving the problem, open negotiations are not difficult to achieve.

I am reminded of a metaphor that is helpful when thinking of dialogue that encourages focused conversation. Couples in healthy dialogue will feel an exchange of expression that's like an easy exchange in playing tennis; lobbing the ball back and forth over the net, the intention being to have a long volley, so the ball is hit in a way that makes it easy for the person on the other side of the net to return the ball. It is not competitive, and you are not looking for that one spot that would be nearly impossible for an "opponent" to race to and successfully return the ball to the other side. Think of playing cooperatively, so the rally is kept going back and forth for as long as this can be accomplished.

Compare this with the game of racquetball. The ball is hit to the front wall but can go anywhere from there. At lightning speed, it careens off in one direction, hits the ceiling, the back wall, a sidewall, the floor. Although it eventually finds its way once again to the front wall, it has been quick and confounding all along. Keeping up with the volley is not predictable. It's chaotic and exciting, but you seldom could sustain the volley for more than a few hits.

This is much like how conversations can be. Upon entering the conversation, if your desire is to have the conversation continue through completion of a subject, then you will do your part to create a flow of dialogue that encourages participation that is easy and desirable. You are not going to provoke a dynamic that would make the conversation chaotic.

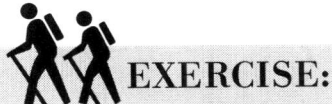 **EXERCISE:**

Even the simple act of jotting down a single-word topic on a piece of paper can help bring focus to a conversation. Create a reminder of the one specific topic of concern prior to beginning the discussion.

Keeping the me/we balance while you're engaged in solving problems takes discipline. But our brains are hard-wired to be at our service. We always can learn new tricks if we are committed to the task.

Commitment To Caring for Each Other

In "An Entire Marriage," *Las Vegas Review-Journal* columnist Steven Kalas writes that when first married, couples often promise they "will give all of themselves to the other." And then, he writes, "in regular intervals of epiphany, often prompted by our mate's protests and indignation, we find ourselves confessing yet another part of ourselves we are withholding from An Entire Marriage." What part of "all of myself" gets retracted?

Finding yourself does not mean that it is not possible for you to couple with another. It means that you dedicate yourself in the relationship to finding a balance that feels just right. Each couple will discover there are many conversations that just didn't occur early in their courting. Many stones remain unturned no matter how thoroughly the couple explored them prior to marriage.

American Neoplatonic writer and public speaker Ken Wilber II described well the later stages of life when he said, "The classic spiritual journey always begins elitist and ends egalitarian." This applies to marriages as well. We begin believing that ours is the most special and unique of relationships, that it holds the greatest possibilities of any we have seen. We see our love through elitist lenses by amplifying the good and diminishing the challenging parts of coming together.

Eventually, however, we discover things about each other that erode this idealized view of our beloved, and we feel that we have been cheated or betrayed. Perhaps we believe that we have been deceived or misled, or that vital information has been withheld. Nevertheless, we feel that it might have made a difference if we had known pertinent information. We couldn't know we were merely experiencing the realities of blending with each other. This is a normal and predictable stage in the evolution of a marriage. It means we still have much to talk and learn about each other. That's all.

Reframing this sense of violation and deceit to one of anticipation helps us come to know each other more truthfully and creates a shift that allows for blissful possibilities. If this is seen as a natural experience in blending the self with the other, then it can be an exciting journey. It won't be comfortable always, but it can be exhilarating.

The rewards of taking this journey are both practical and spiritual. We are enriched when we see the humanity in another person take shape while we discover our own humanity. To live a privileged existence, as if we somehow deserved more or are entitled to more than someone else, is to live in discomfort. There is too much suffering on this planet to think we can raise ourselves up above another human being. It doesn't solve anything and causes much grief.

No one has an easy experience of living on planet Earth. None of us came equipped to complete our life's course without falling many times. To grow as people, we must seek the experience of transitioning from elitist to egalitarian. The process of creating a satisfying union requires that we dive into the me/we paradox. In this quest for balance, we become comfortable in an uncomfortable and stretching process. In the end, we become egalitarian—evenly matched, balanced and coordinated. This only can happen if we escape the prison we build when we insist on exclusively getting our way.

Experts who have researched the subject of connection conclude that the most important bonding emotion is not love but compassion. Compassion compels us to be sensitive to the condition and vulnerability of our partner. It helps us appreciate the differences in temperaments and perspectives and, of course, weaknesses. If we tell our partner, "I want to talk," it might be perceived as an attempt to demean or diminish the partner. But if done with compassion, it can be felt as an attempt to repair a part of the marriage that keeps creating distance, and therefore is actually an attempt to get closer.

Love is an intense emotion, and when it exists, we might erroneously conclude that we merge with our partner, that we see things the same, that we are One. On the other hand, compassion allows us to see the world from different perspectives and helps us to be protective of each other. If you desire your partner to have compassion for you, then it is imperative that you have compassion for your partner.

Here are a few practical ideas about fear that asks for greater compassion:

- Fear and anxiety are heightened during transition states, such as career changes, leaving and coming home, going on vacation, taking a business or personal trip, adding a new child to the family, and the beginning of a new school semester or year.

- Fear of isolation or rejection is more likely to flare up when an emotional connection is strained or broken.

Margaret Johansen, M.S., MFT

- Anything that occurs suddenly, either positive or negative, increases emotional intensity and arousal (the rattlesnake is on alert). Even something so ordinary as interruption by a cell phone ringing can elevate emotional intensity.

- Criticism, or fear of rejection, drives others to someone else in search of support.

Compassion is a quality of character that can be practiced and reinforced, even forcing the eradication of how we previously behaved. For instance, if you formerly were very critical of your husband but now wish to see him through a lens that offers greater compassion, you need to override the critical thoughts that travel through your brain. Patricia Love and Steven Stosny used a visual metaphor in their book, *How To Improve Your Marriage Without Talking About It*. They describe a pile of dirt on the ground prior to a rain. As the rain begins, the first little trails of water descend the mound free to run off in any direction. However, once a path is formed, subsequent water flow increasingly will be more inclined to follow the same path. With time, the path becomes deeper, a rut is formed and it is difficult for water to go down the mound in any direction except following the deep rut. This is very similar to how neural pathways form in our brains and become "permanent" neural connections. If the thought, "My husband is a jerk," is repeated in the mind many times, it is difficult to see your husband any other way. As you repeat this line of thought, the rut becomes deeper.

We expand compassion and learn selflessness. We get out of our own experiences and into the experiences of others. We expand our ability to understand and show compassion. We then can use this ability to bring grace to our own marriages.

 **EXERCISE:**

The most important of all attachment emotions is compassion. This emotion helps us be sensitive to the vulnerability, individuality and depth of our partner.

Try to develop greater compassion within yourself by pushing beyond the Self to understand and ask yourself: "What is my husband's greatest fear and vulnerability?" Often, for men, it is the shame of not succeeding. Women are less fearful about this, because they experience peace in connection to others, so they are not as personally threatened if they don't rise to the top of the career ladder.

OR:

"What is my wife's greatest fear and vulnerability?" Often, the fear for women stems from the weight and anxiety that they might be utterly isolated and alone, leaving them vulnerable to harm, deprivation and isolation. Men are not as vulnerable to this thought, because their esteem comes from succeeding as a provider.

Margaret Johansen, M.S., MFT

Enjoying the Goodness and Pleasure in Life While Affirming the Difficult and Tragic

The world is full of things, small and large, in which an optimistic, hopeful person can take delight—a look, light touching leaves on a tree, a bunny hopping through someone's front yard, a note filled with misspellings from a grandchild. These delights, though small, contribute to a cheerful disposition.

We have to be serious, too. Existential philosophers and others attempt to examine how humans find meaning in their earthly existence. Authors such as Søren Kierkegaard, Martin Buber, Friedrich Nietzsche, St. Teresa of Avila, Jean-Paul Sartre and David Thoreau explore the challenge of finding the self, the meaning of life, free will, choice and personal responsibility. They teach that self-regulation and careful consideration of our actions are crucial to life, because they teach us to discover our own individual natures as we confront our daily struggles. Every decision we make is an ethical one. Our challenge is always to consider our own preferences and desires at the same time we consider the happiness of others and all of humankind.

One of the enduring lessons these authors teach is that human experience is solitary and difficult. With all of its miracles and glory, life is not easy. We only can accept something for what it is. All the efforts we make to reframe dreadful circumstances into something that fits some idealized framework are doomed to be futile.

Life is not to be easy, nor are relationships. Important relationships challenge our expectations of others and ourselves. They force us to face the unappealing aspects of our humanity. We all desire love and intimacy but the price for love and intimacy is that we must accept that we live a paradox. We may want to live in "an entire marriage," yet, to do so, we have to give up the parts of our being that drive us to hold back for the sake of controlling what cannot be controlled. There's the paradox! It is a hard task and, sometimes, it hurts. But, it stretches and enriches us.

A client recently described a family loss she suffered in the past year. Her father-in-law, who was beloved by her and her entire family, had died of a serious infection following surgery. After a series of unexpected complications, each robbing just a little more life from this cherished individual, death suddenly crushed all hope of an anticipated recovery. Seven months later, this beautiful woman still is caught in the throes of loss, compounded by the grief she felt from never really having said good-bye.

At first, we shed tears that validated her loss. Then we recounted what was good in her life, particularly her good fortune. We noticed the depth of love and joy she felt as she recounted experiences that had left indelible memories. Simultaneously, she also discovered the penetrant sting of loss. They are two sides of the same coin; they cannot be separated. They are normal feelings in our lives.

Margaret Johansen, M.S., MFT

Loss comes to us in so many ways. Death may catch us off guard and be a mightily unwelcome surprise. An unstable economy dashes dreams for many people who have relentlessly worked at a business only to find that nothing more can be done to save it. Committed relationships end, not always mutually. Some people have to leave a home because of financial hardship or war and try to build a new life in another location. Others face the suicide of a child or other loved one. Parents stand by powerless when their child pursues a life choice that threatens harm. The list of compelling losses is unending.

Often, instead of accepting these tragedies, people stick their heads in the sand and look for distractions. Many turn to compulsive behavior as a way of refusing to adjust to the tragedies of life. Compulsions such as over-shopping, over-eating, over-reading, gambling, over-spending, over-socializing, addiction to sex, alcohol, drugs, food or electronic games, and obsessive neediness are often provoked by discomfort with the tragic. In our aloneness, rather than spending time to understand the pain and seeking to learn from it, we engage in dysfunctional behaviors to numb ourselves. In the short term, such distractions indeed may help us feel we are not alone. They ease the pain of being alone and help us feel better ... temporarily. But the pain always returns. If we do not face it, and give it the attention and healing it needs, we are likely to engage in yet another compulsive episode to cover up the painful emotions once again. This cycle will repeat again and again until we give up the short-term fixes and address our deeper needs.

Marriage is hardly tragic, yet even in marriage we see the same behaviors. If partners embrace the difficult or uncomfortable feelings they experience in their marriages and speak to each other about these feelings, they would need no short-term fixes. Blaming the other is a short-term fix. Arguing triggered by anger or defensive stances is a form of short-term balm; it lets a person feel assertive and powerful in the short-term but does little to resolve the underlying imbalances or problems. Like compulsive gambling or drinking, arguing is a compulsive attempt to avoid better long-term solutions—real communication, commitment to the relationship, awareness and critical thinking without accusation.

Letting Go ... Really, Truly, Deeply Letting Go

Long, intimate or entwined relationships affect us deeply. Especially when we have shared goals that blend mutual careers, child rearing, and hopes and dreams, we experience merging. We become a part of each other. We think, not just about ourselves, but also about how our partner thinks and feels. Our thoughts and feelings become entwined. Scientific findings suggest that even our biologies merge.

When some trauma occurs in the marriage, we experience challenge in all these areas. It affects all the ways we are connected to our partner: emotionally, spiritually and biologically. Our feelings are magnified by the fact that it is not just anyone who betrayed us but our significant other.

Steve and Danielle are a young couple who had their first child just nine months ago. Although they have been married six years, Danielle has yet to work out her relationship with Steve's family. She feels subservient to Ellen, Steve's sister. She believes his opinionated sister has more influence over matters between her and Steve than she should have. Steve tried to reassure her that he respects the boundaries of their marriage. He strongly has communicated with his sister in an effort to quiet her imposing voice. He confronted both his sister and his parents about their meddling in areas that were private and personal between him and his wife.

But, this wasn't enough. A remark Ellen had made three years earlier continues to echo in Danielle's mind. Danielle overheard Ellen say that, were Steve and Danielle ever to divorce, Ellen would be on her brother's side. Even though Ellen had made this inappropriate comment long ago, it continues to haunt the couple. They talk about it, even argue about it, three or four times per week. This occurs in spite of the fact that Steve has discussed the problem with his sister; she has apologized and said that she will be far more careful in what she flippantly says. In Ellen's experience, the damage has been done. Steve and Danielle infrequently have seen Ellen since this occurred and never for more than one or two days at a time. Today Danielle does not want Ellen to have any contact with their young daughter, because she feels her sister-in-law would be a negative influence on the child.

The amount of distress Steve and Danielle have suffered contending with one another about Ellen's one thoughtless sentence is heartbreaking. Steve continues, to no avail, to make genuine efforts to define and defend their family boundaries. Danielle continues to have a very difficult time letting go. Both of them struggle to define what family loyalty is and how it can be expressed. Until Ellen can let go of what has become a near hatred, it seems highly unlikely that deep resolution of this situation can occur.

Peggy's experience is completely different. Throughout her 50 years of life, her mother has been mostly critical toward her. Peggy endured an extended and acrimonious divorce, yet her mother continued visiting her former son-in-law, and attending parties and holiday celebrations with his family, all in disregard of the hurt her behavior caused her own daughter. Peggy sought therapy to help her cope with the abuse and learn to establish dignified boundaries. She now can stand up to her mother's requests and demands while still treating her mother with grace and regard.

With my encouragement, Peggy wrote a letter to her mother, explaining why and how the mother's behavior caused Peggy pain. Her mother's reply was, "Get over it." She didn't apologize or offer any indication that she related to how Peggy felt. Recognizing that her mother long has been her greatest critic, Peggy has distanced herself yet a bit further from her mother. She still finds opportunities to be with her mother and attempts to forge a more supportive relationship. She is realistic about the prospects. She knows she'll never enjoy the closeness she has longed for throughout the years. She has accepted that she can mother herself even while she loves her mother. She has set boundaries that do not bring injury and she has let go of the idealized vision of what she wanted her mother to be. She accepts the mother she has. Peggy has found an honest, graceful and respectful path that is landscaped with as much kindness as she can find for herself and her mother. The evolution has been beautiful.

Sometimes letting go means redefining. It often requires turning off the brain's predilection to think random, destructive thoughts that, in the long term, damage the Self. Letting go allows a person to reclaim their agency—the internal capacity to choose thoughts and behaviors and not let unquestioned thoughts and behaviors run one's life. Letting go frees a person from being tyrannized by long-ago mistreatments that still victimize the Self. Letting go requires each of us to pick up the dead weight we've been carrying, to throw it aside, to stand up tall and to redirect our personal thoughts to serve our lives better.

Chapter 5

The Gifts
of Generosity
and Grace

The various skills and lessons of the first four chapters converge beneath the protective umbrella of generosity and grace. With this presence, working with the neuro-biology of the brain, listening with intention to understand, playfulness and merging of the I/We transforms a marriage into a work of art. The desire of the human spirit to be understood and valued is given a place of respect. Without these qualities, all that we learn and practice is less prolific with vital possibility for the exquisite vitality it can bring to our lives.

Webster defines 'generosity' as "freedom from meanness or smallness of mind or character'; 'Largeness or fullness, readiness or liberality in giving. Some synonyms might be: charity, benevolence, unselfishness.

'Grace' means "elegance or beauty of form, manner, or action." "A manifestation of favor, goodwill or kindness." And, some synonyms might be, "finesse, consideration, balance, dignity."

Assumptions

In America, we live in a society that emphasizes doing and achieving. Most of us lead very busy lives, filled with scheduled appointments and tasks, feeling a chronic sense of under-performance in one area or another. We typically feel 'behind' on something, living with a sense of things undone that we wish were done. Seemingly, the solution for this is to devote less time to something: sleep, time with spouse, time with children, exercise or personal time, home or property upkeep, etc. The hope is that finding a few minutes here or there will help us liberate the additional time needed to accomplish something we feel deserves increased attention. Always juggling.

Ashanti is a client who has recently transitioned through a divorce. It has not been a calm transition and she is left feeling destitute even though she is a capable professional woman. Even though she earns a reliable income, it has been financially very difficult for her. Ashanti finds herself less able to maintain the focus she has relied on to be productive in her work. Her mind just spins with 'craziness' (her term), as thoughts whip through at lightning speed: "How can I get him completely out of my mind so I can focus?" Her immediate feeling of panic began the day prior to our meeting, as she declined taking a large contract job because she just didn't feel she could focus to accomplish the work. In addition to providing for the needs of her own current and future life, she carries the weight of contributing to graduate education for one of her children while the other child serves a humanitarian mission in another country. Ashanti finds all of this so overwhelming that she is unable to focus clearly and consistently — she feels that she is in a chronic state of panic.

Ashanti's ability to slow down and give focused attention to a task at hand feels momentarily broken. What she has always believed to be reliable in her life is now far less dependable. Spinning thoughts consume her, generating animated body language, wide-eyed facial expression. All of these are typical signs of fear. She sought therapy because she knew her fear consumed her, rendering her incapable of thinking clearly about how she could help herself manage this situation.

I tell this story, because we see it often in each other. The panic that comes because of feeling overwhelmed, feeling that there is just no "strength from within" to muscle-up with! We believe a resolution could be found if we could just try harder, create, implement, struggle, exert, or carry on. But, fear raises its head when there is nothing more to do that with.

Can you relate to a time when your spouse initiated a discussion? Rather than bringing focus and a spirit of goodwill with intention to understand, did you too quickly jump to the conclusion that an argument was brewing? Did an internal whirlwind of thought begin, causing emotions to elevate somewhat even before you had cause for this to happen? Can you think of a time when you did not respond to a question or comment with generosity of presence and desire to understand? Can you imagine how this might sometimes amplify the overwhelmed and fearful feeling that your spouse is already feeling?

The dictionary defines the word *assumption* as "taking something for granted; something expected." It is interesting that the antonyms are "genuineness, reality, naturalness." Assumptions might be contrived, based in distortion or ignorance. Many times, what is familiar is experienced just as this professional woman experienced—fear, chaos, uncertainty. Even with the greatest skill we might develop to try to avoid them, we will never run out of assumptions! All that can be brought is one's best intention to be present with their spouse, to try to listen wholeheartedly, and try to be neutral while listening occurs. If assumptions are a part of the normal human tendency, then it requires constant vigilance to speak and listen honestly. It requires that we always be on alert to discern obstacles to heartfelt gift of grace and objectivity in any circumstance. It is difficult to not spew opinions of rebuttal or defense that have the impact of pushing against everything that counters them. That's what assumptions do to us.

I want to stop here to tell a tory. It has nothing to do with couples, but with a little girl who happens to be my granddaughter. Mayli was visiting me in the Las Vegas area when she was 10 years old. We had a sweet day together, walking through the magnificent hotel properties downtown. While at the Venetian Hotel, we stopped at the side of the indoor canal to listen to the beautiful tenor voice of one of the gondola guides. As we stood near the wall that separated the walkway from the waterway, I had my arm around Mayli's shoulder and we were absorbed in another world. From somewhere, the tiniest voice said, "Little Girl?" I barely heard it, but did not at first turn to see its source. Then, just barely louder, the soft voice once again said, "Little Girl?" Still hardly hearing it, I happened to turn my head. To my amazement, there was a most beautiful woman dressed in ornate clothes of heavy velvet. Her hair was in precise ringlets, and makeup gave her a perfect facial finish. I literally gasped, and touched Mayli's shoulder to guide her attention to this otherworldly young woman. Completely caught off guard, Mayli's response was the same as mine had been — she gasped! At that moment, a small adult hand clothed in a long-sleeved white glove reached out towards Mayli. It held a gold foil wrapped chocolate coin, which the woman offered to Mayli, "Little Girl. Would you like a chocolate?" Mayli reached out to receive the coin, still in disbelief. Just a few seconds of short exchanges were spoken, and the woman disappeared into the crowd. But, Mayli's remarks to me are priceless and memorable, "Grandma! How did she <u>know</u> I was a good girl?" In her mind (her assumptions), this beautiful woman had singled her out because Mayli makes diligent effort to be 'good' and this woman somehow knew and rewarded Mayli's effort.

This is *precisely* the message I want to convey. Assumptions can lift us and reinforce our character. Mayli's mind used that circumstance to reinforce her belief that she tries hard to make ethical choices. As married partners, it is important that we look for opportunities to make kind gestures that validate the worth of our partner. It is imperative that we are vigilant in monitoring and understanding assumptions we have about ourselves and also those we make about others.

 **EXERCISE:**

Divide a sheet of paper in half lengthwise, so you have two large columns. At the head of the left side, write the word "Positive", and the right side will be 'Negative'. Write descriptive words and phrases that you believe describe you. These will not all be glowing and positive. But, try to be very honest. The list is exclusively for you, not for any other eyes to see.

Margaret Johansen, M.S., MFT

When you have finished writing these short words and phrases, please take a moment to jot down some notes of times you have behaved differently. So, what behaviors have you demonstrated that counters or goes against the descriptive phrase. Do this for both the Positive and the Negative side of the paper.

The purpose of this is merely to find a balanced, honest appraisal of our Self.

A friend of mind has two daughters and two sons. He was speaking of his 16-year old daughter today, and commented that he doesn't call her by her given name, which is Ann. He said, I call her by her *full* name — which is Annie Banani Big Bucket of Love sent from Heaven Above. It's a funny name, for sure. However, can you imagine what the cumulative impact of this has been over her childhood years? It carries such welcome and appreciation in having her as part of their family. This is the kind of humanity and generosity I am speaking about — that is needed for husbands and wives. A husband or wife has opportunity for significant impact on the growth of the other person.

Unfortunately, we can also have great impact in discounting the worth of the other. And, our minds can use these repetitive negative messages from a spouse to conclude worthlessness. Rita and Lance are both police officers. Rita was raised in a family where aggressiveness was the normal way of functioning. Rapid and loud speech was the family standard and, if you did not compete for being heard in that way, you wouldn't be heard. Imagine how this elevated tone now sounds in normal, everyday marriage conversation. Lance believes that his wife was constantly being demeaning towards him. He appreciated that she is strong-willed and capable, because it allows him to not worry about her as she is out in the community in her service as a police detective. But, he surely finds offense at her tone of voice with him at home!

I spoke to these two people about thinking of their marriage as a 'container', a vessel that would hold a variety of emotional states and moods. Within this place would be a sense of welcome, embrace, and support. It would be a place where each could bring successes, vulnerabilities, celebrations, and the deepest and even darkest places of their respective joys and fears. Most especially, each would contribute to shaping a relationship that would support the healing and growth of the other, by honoring the humanness each brings to the marriage.

This takes grace and strong intention. Because, sometimes the human impulse IS to treat one's wife or husband like a knucklehead. But, being human, by definition, means being imperfect and in need of refinement. Over a lifetime of years lived together, we hope to create something which has the strength to withstand the various stresses that the marriage will face. That strength is woven with grace, love, and respect.

Margaret Johansen, M.S., MFT

Look at the power of assumptions; assumptions lift us and help reinforce our character. And, assumptions bring us down. Mayli's mind used that circumstance to reinforce her effort in living moral behaviors. Lance and Rita found that assumptions reinforced a negative belief. All come from the same source — our own minds. Assumptions are born from some part of what we already believe within ourselves!

Expectations

The dictionary explains the meaning of this word, expectation, as "to look forward to; regard as likely to happen. To look for with reason or justification." It sets the stage, from the information *believed to be accurate and reliable*, for us to think something will happen. The italics highlight the vulnerability of expectations, because often it is the inaccuracy of the information, or miscommunication of information, that creates inaccurate expectations.

Once inaccurate or miscommunicated information has set an expectation in place, too often the expectance is quite rigid. Often, couples find that it has been set as an absolute, and no reason or excuse ameliorates the intensity of what is expected. Of course, on some critical matters, this is understandable. But, in the little everyday miscommunications, it is curious that unmet expectations become such a large issue. Surely, something else drives those exaggerated responses. When the violation of the offense is compared against the intensity of reaction, it can't be because of a forgotten assignment to purchase a dozen eggs! I believe it goes back to the survival instincts spoken about in chapter 1, that it is somehow 'proof' of unfulfilled love, and a lack of feeling worth. If you agree with this, you might return to the first two chapters of this book, and reconsider how this dynamic is currently functioning in your marriage.

Taking a short detour here, I would like to evaluate how business owners track expectations through the operation of their company. Most often, successful business owners have a structure of operation that includes a way to identify, clarify, and track expectations. This can be accomplished by some template or form, passed along through auto scanning the process as it travels along the prescribed pathway. Or, it can merely be initials on a sheet of paper that accompanies an assignment or item of merchandise. Interviews are held to ascertain if the job description is understood, if the expectation of the job description is being fulfilled, therefore, achieving the standard set forth by the clearly communicated parameters.

In addition, interviews are scheduled. It can be in the form of a very short meeting, just to check up on the fulfillment of completion. Or, it can be a scheduled quarterly interview, wherein there is a review of how a person is performing when compared to the requirements of specified expectations. All of these are an effort of a well-honed company to define, clarify, communicate, adjust, and achieve expectations.

Margaret Johansen, M.S., MFT

Expectations in intimate relationships grow from our needs to be seen, understood, listened to, and cared about. Early in the dating process, we more often bring focused attention as we listen to each other. Our expressions are animated and involved. We listen with interest and enthusiasm. As life together progresses along, distractions multiply, and it becomes easy to pay less attention to our partner's need to be seen, understood, listened to, and cared about.

When this kind of tracking is compared to how couples typically communicate expectation, it is little wonder that so much mis-communication occurs. It is common that there would be a dialogue that goes something like this:

Wife: "Will you please stop at the store on the way home and pick up cream cheese, eggs, celery, and pasta?"

Husband: "Sure, I'd be happy to. I'll see you later, around 5."

So, when he comes home, he has cream, cheddar cheese, eggs, celery, and pasta in the grocery bag. The ensuing conversation sounds like this:

Wife: "What is this? This isn't what I asked for..."

Husband: "It absolutely is. I know I heard you say that you wanted cream, cheese, eggs, celery, and pasta. What are you upset about?"

Wife: "I can't believe you didn't get cream cheese, it is clearly what I asked for. Why don't you listen better? Do you have wax in your ears!"

Or, you might think that this is an easy mis-communication, because at least the husband heard the words correctly. What about when the husband asks the wife to please get the oil changed in the car? And, the wife does not even register that this request was made of her. So, this leaves the husband with the expectation that some specific task will get done. And, the wife has no such expectation of herself that day. Imagine how easily this kind of misunderstanding could be avoided. It can, with just one very simple technique.

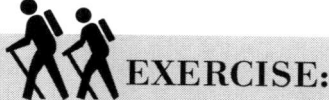

EXERCISE:

Commit, from this time on, to repeat exactly what you heard when it comes to 'requests or assignments.' Use respectful and clarifying language that reflects what you just thought you heard. For instance, if the husband asks his wife to please have an oil change done on the car, she will merely say back to him, "You would like me to get the oil changed in the car. Does that need to be done today, or is tomorrow OK." If he doesn't hear her repeat the request back to him, she apparently didn't hear the request. It's OK to repeat the request, in that case.

Inner Argument with Life

Assumptions can have such influence, that they become a signature banner that helps shape our life. This can be powerful, either in a positive influence or in a negative way. Some carry the banner of <u>persecution,</u> with ongoing stories of ill treatment from others. They watch for it, are extra-sensitive to this dynamic, and have a laundry list in their soul of how Life has battered them with large and small injustices. Others carry a testament for <u>entitlement</u>. They lead their life in a manner that expects their basic needs to be provided for by others. They can be angry and resentful if these expectations are unmet. Until these people discover and embrace their own power and assume responsibility for choices in their lives, they are victim to decisions and behavior of others. There are those who have an ongoing dialogue of <u>rationalization</u>, looking to find one excuse after another why they are unable to work towards their interests and desires — or even their passions. There always will be some external reason why they cannot obtain what they most want, but it seldom has anything to do with them. These paradigms permeate the relationship with every person. With all of these opinions and judgments, it is difficult to experience wonder and amazement. Minds are just too busy defending, rationalizing and rejecting.

I discover grace and generosity as I seek to mix the specific difficulties of my own life with the larger essence of humankind. I find stability as I walk along a trail, noticing composite rock that has sediment pieces from many other rocks and minerals and places and times. I am reminded of the mystery of my own life, as I realize that meteors have pelleted our Earth, depositing dust of other stars in the ground upon which I now walk. When I slow down and feel the weight of a current trial mixed in the immensity of the balance that sustains my fragile life, I can feel gratitude coexisting along with what I am suffering with. It abides all in the same moment — together. One does not discredit the other, just brings balance to any problem.

I viewed a YouTube video, "Lightning in A Jar". It is a reminder of how fortunate we are. If you are even holding this book, can read, have a roof over your head and food in the refrigerator, a little money in your pocket and funds in a bank account, your life is more privileged than most people who are currently alive. If you have an education and can worship in a place where you don't worry about ambush, you have great fortune. We comprise a very small portion of the people currently living on the Earth, if we have all of these things. Let's monitor our thoughts and remember to be thankful, along with the hardships.

Letting go

Assumptions involve distortion and self-importance. A problem with these identifications is that they get in the way. Even if there is an element of truth in the story that actuates an assumption, the assumption itself generates distortion. For instance, if I believe people will persecute me because of my religious affiliation, then I will be hypersensitive to both inflections of voice or body language from other people — and I will interpret those variances to give evidence that I am being persecuted. Notice that the focus is entirely on MY experience, not the experience of the other. Mark Nepo writes, 'If I am ever to glimpse the world outside the stubborn certainty of the mind, we have to put down our ready answer to everything." Assumptions are part of that ready answer. It creates a pre-existing condition to any observation or conversation.

The fact is that Life will unravel us time after time throughout our journey. This intends no pessimism, but is descriptive of the landscape of just being alive. It is how we are transformed. As we become broken, we are sometimes afraid of treading back into a situation that appears to have similarities to what broke us the first time. But, we all have been broken. We all have difficulties in our Life Story. Most of us carry hurt from someone's self-interest, the crushing of something that was held dear. Some suffer the stabbing pain of the loss of a child or the loss of hopes for that child. Many feel attacked by slanderous comments said in a moment of meanness by another. There are broken promises and twisted narratives that cause great pain. Some grieve from the effort given with grace and goodwill, but rebutted by actions of unspeakable meanness broadcast through families and friends. All of this breaks us down.

But, what breaks us down also contains the golden nuggets of our transformation and growth. There is beauty within the pain and happiness in the heartache. It is possible to distill soothing nectar from the pain and to build hope and character from the worst that life has delivered to us.

Knowing this to be true, not only for me, but for everyone, I can find grace, generosity, and compassion. When I allow my experiences of life to enlarge compassion within, I am blessed with a greater abundance of benevolence, empathy, kindness, softheartedness, friendliness, charity, and grace. I can bring this greater quality to my overall perspective of living daily life. Most particularly, I can bring an improved sense of peacefulness and poise to the marriage I care so deeply about.

A very bright and capable 66-year-old gentleman sat in my office. He has been a fire fighter, by profession. However, now retired, he has much more time to spend being with his wife of many years and working around their home and garden. In the transition of his retirement, it has become apparent to him how much he acquiesces to all of his wife's requests, and how incapable he seems to be in asserting his own preferences. As we were exploring this subject, he told a simple story. It is simple, but also very profound in ways neither of us imagined as he began telling it.

His parents divorced when he was very young, around the age of 4. This necessitated that his mother seek employment, not just one job, but three. His sister who was three years his senior cared for him most of the time his mother was at work. Neither child saw their father very much following the divorce. So, in essence, they lost two parents and an intact family. Within the next few years, the one time of year where hope and joy was restored was around the Christmas holiday. My client told that he loved the sparkling lights on the tree, and the few gifts tied in glittery bows. Especially meaningful was the fact that the family was reunited on Christmas Day. It was just like old times, Mom and Dad together and the children embraced in a family who played and enjoyed each other.

One December, when this now grown man was six years old, the mother came in after a particularly trying and long day of work, and made an appeal to him, "You don't really need all of that Christmas stuff up this year, do you? You really don't need it, right?" He noticed the pleading look on her face, and realized that she just had no more to give. So, he swallowed his own desires for what had become symbolic of possibility and hope, and responded that it was fine to not decorate for this special holiday. That was it — the end of speaking up for himself. Achieved by one innocent comment from his mother in a way that left an imprint that remained strong for the next 60 years. The label he believed defined him was, "I don't deserve to have what I want." Not only had he learned to believe this early in his life, but also his wife learned to accommodate that label. Now, he realizes that his Argument with Life is that Life did not deliver what he most wanted for himself. He also realizes, that it is up to him to make necessary changes to ensure the possibility that he <u>can</u> have more of what he desires for himself.

The task is to develop the ability to listen and receive with grace, rather than to observe and manipulate. Much of the rejection or isolation we each feel is the counter-effect of living an Argument with Life.

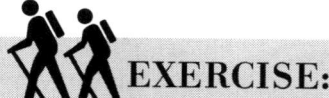 **EXERCISE:**

Make a list of the Arguments you have with Life. List just 5 ways in which you resent how life has gone for you so far. Specifically, list 5 elements in your life that you are unhappy with right now. Perhaps some of these you are currently working on, or have invested a lot of effort into changing in the past. Maybe there are unsatisfying areas of your life that you just cannot do anything about. Just list 5.

1. _____

2. _____

3. _____

4. _____

5. _____

Now choose just one that you are willing to let go of. You will not grumble about this any more. You will make effort that seems reasonable to keep moving towards transition or evolution, but you will let go of your bitter feelings about this. Done. Now do it....

Margaret Johansen, M.S., MFT

EXERCISE #2:

Repeat this same exercise, only this time the list of 5 will be about grievances you hold in your heart towards your partner. List 5 things that bother you. Spend some time thinking about this, because you will, once again, be letting go of one of the 5. You have the strength and determination to do this. It's only 1 thing...Let it go. Forever. It is an act of Grace for both of you. I assure you that you will be amazed and thankful for the relief this brings to your marriage.

One of my several treasures is a Tibetan Singing Bowl. I was told that this particular bowl is made of 9 different metals: gold, silver, lead, tin, copper, mercury, iron and meteorite elements. It has been formed into the bowl shape by hand hammering; so little indentations are visible upon close inspection. I love it, not only for the harmonics created by the metal alloys, but also just for its look. It reminds me of Life. I feel hammered sometimes. Hammered doesn't need to mean blasted apart. In the case of the singing bowl, and I hope also in Life, hammered means formed and refined into something beautiful. Let me, and you, as the bowl, shine and sing our song of Life.

The masterful Eric Fromm spoke of love as 'the active power that breaks through the walls that separate one human from another...uniting us with one another." This is the great love that needs to become the standard of life for each of us. This love holds the generosity and grace that we need to share with each other. This kind of love helps still our minds, brings a greater presence to our marriage, and embraces the humanity of our spouse. This humanity stems from knowing absolutely that we are all broken, we are all striving, and we all are learning and growing. There is no one who has mastered all of this process. We each journey with the hope that, at the end of our lives, we will look back upon the experience and how it has formed us and will say it has been worth it. We will say that we have appreciated and loved Life.

How to Still The Mind

I believe the mind is stilled using two qualities: intention and discipline. Intention to quiet the mind is born of the desire to be more generous and give grace towards the spouse. In even a larger context, it is borne of the desire to enlarge the capacity to listen to everyone, and to Life. It is the effort to quiet the repetitive and largely negative thoughts that automatically run around in our minds. It is the desire to bring a greater sense of safety to the marriage. It is the hope that we can protect against hurting others intentionally.

This work is based on seeing the other as someone who is human; broken, beautiful, naïve, wise, evolving. Whatever is said or whatever the action, the work is to just be still with it *first*. Our inherited hardwiring would compel us to react and behave differently. Discipline is the quality that brings desired change. Without impulsive and unreasonable response, just let it sit in the space of your body and mind for a few minutes. If the brain constructs reactive words, push them aside and instruct the brain that you will get back to it later, if needed. If hormones flood to the extremities of the body, compelling quick unmediated action, instruct them to do something else. Perhaps you go for a walk or at least give distance to the person who provoked such a reaction within you. Use discipline to maintain the space within yourself needed to find stillness of mind.

The comfort we feel with what is familiar runs deep. Please understand that being still as a first response will initially feel awkward. Please give it a try, anyway. Stillness is what allows for the opening of generosity towards all others. It is what makes way for grace to fill our hearts and work its way into our marriage relationships. It is what grows intimacy and closeness.

As we do this, we make room for impulses of the Soul to surface. Rather than allowing the mind's reactions control thoughts and behavior, we make room for the Soul's response to Life. You will discover that these are not the same. The impulses of the mind can often sabotage our most beloved relationships. The impulses of the Soul are clear and direct. We can learn to recognize them when they are felt. The impulses of the Soul cry out for what is True for us.

They will guide us on a pathway that enables evolution and growth.

The impulses of the mind more often adhere to what is familiar, even at the expense of growth. If we react on the impulses of the mind, the aspects of familiar, repetitious behavior are strengthened.

We *need* an honest partner who will give us very needed feedback and even correction. Otherwise, it is too easy to believe the neurotic thoughts of our own mind, which reinforce all that is familiar and safe, but often sabotages us.

One of my closest woman friends, Melanie, was left with 7 children and a small Honda Civic. This wasn't in the year 2013, when Civics is more accommodating vehicles. This was back in the 1980s, when a Honda Civic was about the same size as a roller skate! This dear woman had limited ability to earn a living sufficient to support a family. She feared that she would loose not only her husband, but also her home. And, she was afraid that, if this should happen, she would not be able to provide for her children.

Intense feelings of fear and panic rose up, and Melanie became fearful that she would be incapable of working through this tremendous adversity in her life. We walked together sometimes in the early morning hours. As we walked, we shared moments of quiet, during which we pondered possible solutions. Stilling the mind. During our walks, (1) I just listened and allowed all of her emotions to have a place of respect and validity, (2) I could acknowledge and contain the permissibility of all that she felt, and (3) I had some ideas, but didn't take on the task of trying to solve this seemingly insurmountable problem.

I believe this is the essence of loving ourselves and other people — that we bring our full capacity to listening. We intend to use every faculty of presence to be with the other person in their time of need or despair. We don't skirt away from this task, nor do we involve ourselves in a way that amplifies the 'drama' of it. We just support and bring heart and soul to the situation. Secondly, we allow emotion to genuinely be what it is. This takes practice. When a loved one is consumed in the intensity of emotion — as was my friend in this occasion — it is difficult to just stay present with a person and all of the variety of emotions they feel: Anger, fear, despair, helplessness. All of these emotions felt with a depth and intensity that is hard to bear. Still, in loving, we stay. If there is anger, we can listen and paraphrase the content of the words without taking in that same emotion. If there is fear, we can acknowledge it without letting the fear overwhelm us or the other person with disproportionate intensity. If there is despair, we allow it long enough that it is honored, but not so long so that it begins to define the person.

We bring our own wisdom and grace to each unique circumstance and are a support, even as intense as these emotions may be. As we generate grace and generosity, we can help provide a context that is welcoming and safe. The relationship becomes capable of creating comfort and renewal.

We are opened by love and awestruck by beauty — both elements that cause us to expand. This expansion stabilizes us when there is pain and fear. We acknowledge that pain and fear just "*is*"a significant part of life. As we bring generosity and compassion to the experience of living, that is called LOVE.

Epilogue

I am reminiscing tonight. Tomorrow, I take this manuscript to the final layout edit prior to sending it off to press. It was in my mind today as I worked with couples and individual clients. Two of these couples are doing so much better in their marriages. They have worked on the principles presented in this book, have learned to speak to each other with grace and respect. I have watched a softening of their love as they have created a marriage that has more openness for each. For one couple in particular, the husband was 'just done' when they initially came to see me a few months ago. He is exhausted with his life of trying to own and operate a small restaurant. And, the wife is exhausted because they have two very young children that are her daily stewardship. Those overwhelming responsibilities are unchanged. But, their manner of communication and the kindness they exhibit for each other has changed. They may still loose their home. But, I know they will not loose each other. They have chosen to hold on, to listen, to offer the best of who they are to each other. This is the reason I wrote this book.

I hope it can help even a few people to bring the best they have to their marriage. I desire to contribute to unions and couplings and love and grace. I do believe an increase of all of this would benefit our planet and our lives. I again leave this message with you, closing with the words of Tiny Tim, "God Bless us Every One."

Biography

Margaret Johansen, a licensed Marriage and Family Therapist with a private practice in Henderson, Nevada, has been helping individuals and couples for more than 18 years. The U.S. Commerce Association has awarded three-times Margaret the Best Individual and Marriage Therapist in Henderson, Nevada. She believes this is largely due to her ongoing passion to synthesize the cutting-edge scientific findings related to brain function with how it translates into human behavior.

The greatest personal gift from being involved in the lives of others as a therapist is a sense of 'evenness' that has evolved within Margaret. She understands that life often requires all that we have, and then pulls for more. Problems that surface in marriages and families can be daunting, for sure. Yet, Margaret believes there is an underlying Life Support that thrives and continues to bubble with joy. There exists the possibility of finding happiness, even as we experience heartache. There is grace and love in difficulty.

Most of us have experienced large and small failures many times, as we continue to strive to succeed. The greatest success lies in the courage; motivation and tenacity to keep on striving as we simultaneously create many moments for relaxation and play.

Margaret Johansen grew up in Shadow Hills, California. Identifying characteristics of her parents were (1) hard work, (2) self-responsibility, and (3) solutions have to work for everyone, not just an individual person. Entering high school in the '60s in a school of more than 6,000 students also heightened this sense of fairness and equity. A time in history rampant with racial tensions and social instability, Margaret set out on a journey to contribute to stability and peace. It has been ongoing ever since that time.

Being a middle child in a family of 7 siblings built the role of balancing relationships. It required learning to negotiate squabbles, reducing friction, ameliorating tension, enhancing communication towards understanding, asking thought-provoking questions, and seeking solutions. The role relates to evenness and stability.

Margaret's older sister was strict, absolute, and vocally opinionated. Her next younger brother was a vocal leader in Vietnam War protests. So, you can imagine the relational pressure cooker that the in-between child experienced!

This beginning in childhood is also the beginning of what compelled Margaret to be a continual seeker in understanding the dynamics of how a relationship works. What makes some very successful, wherein continued friendship and passion are a daily part of a couple's lives? And, in contrast, why do so many relationships deconstruct?

Marrying at age 21, the beginning of a family of five children began one year later. Living at a distance from family of origin, Margaret began the incredible journey of raising children. With a husband whose career path was characterized by customary instability, pressures of raising a family was, at times, profound. She sought to contribute a measure of dependability to family finances by opening a Montessori Early Childhood Education Center in a large room above the garage area of their family home. Enriched by the delight and passion that young children brought daily into her life, Margaret observed first-hand the raw joy of learning inherent in small children. She also grew to believe that this joy is the birthright of every living person, even as we age and as pressures mount. As the late Roger Ebert wrote: "We must try to contribute joy to the world. That is true no matter what our problems, our health, our circumstances. We must try. I didn't always know this and am happy I lived long enough to find it out." Whether working with young children, couples, individuals, families, or homeless people, Margaret still believes in this mission and possibility!

Raising five children, two sons and three daughters, has been an unsurpassed joy in her life. Early in their lives, the joy of education became an integral part of family living. Nature provided a rich schoolhouse, and hours were spent outdoors. If a spider web were discovered, all would return home and learn about spiders. If we walked past a beehive, then the study of bees would emerge. Blue herons engaged in a mating ritual across the street catapulted us into yet another few hours of study. Beautiful hawks in flight far above the valley inspired curious investigation. The wonder of life was plentiful in the Johansen household.

Returning to school at age 44, Margaret pursued a second Bachelor's Degree at Weber State University in Ogden, Utah. She earned a degree in Family Science, and was awarded the Outstanding Student of that college at graduation. Favorite professors, Randy Chatelain, PhD and Craig Campbell, PhD were also marriage therapists. Fond hours of mentoring took place during her schooling there. These guided her towards a decision to attend a graduate program that would continue to expand her understanding about relationships, not only to possibly help her own situation, but also to renovate and brighten relationships for others.

Herself going through a divorce that fractured a family of five children and a 24-year marriage, Margaret immediately went straight to graduate school in Marriage and Family Therapy. There, Margaret discovered a new depth of resource and information that she had not known previously. This flamed into a passion for helping other couples achieve in ways that she had not been able to. Some of the information she discovered was amazing, replete with realizations that would change her life. Growing in astonishment that this information was not, at that time, generally available to the public, Margaret determined to simplify these findings in a way that could be easily understood.

Following suma cum laude graduation from the University of Nebraska-Lincoln with a Masters Degree in Marriage and Family Therapy, Margaret moved with the youngest three of her five children to the Las Vegas Valley. She has worked in several different environments, beginning with a holistic medical clinic wherein Margaret sought to help people find insight into the emotional components of what contributed to their long-term, ongoing illness. Following that internship, Margaret worked at two therapy clinics as she simultaneously began to build a private practice.

Still impassioned by the gnawing sense that the discoveries in the field of brain function and neuroscience held some significant morsels of indispensible information that could transform relationships, Margaret enrolled in a PhD program to learn even more about this essential research.

Interruptions of every sort slowed the process of earning a degree, including the long-term care of aging parents who have since passed on. Near the end of her parent's lives, Margaret made weekly treks from Nevada to Southern California to contribute, along with all of her siblings, to their needs. With the satisfaction of a job well done, there is now greater understanding of the circumstances that sometimes arise in this 'in-between' generation stage. Another piece of understanding and compassion was set in stone.

All the while, the family has added members, and there are now eleven grandchildren who embellish Margaret's life. Sometimes torn that she cannot attend every birthday or school function because if the distances that separate her from these precious children, she prioritizes keeping in touch with them and building solid relationships. Another dimension of love is added to life – it keeps on growing!

Today, Johansen works at her private office, working with clients and relating complex scientific information in an enjoyable, easy-to-understand fashion that has light bulbs going off in heads everywhere. Through individual therapy sessions, presentations to small groups, and speaking engagements that involve hundreds, Margaret still seeks to transform your love and your life!

Testaments

Margaret Johansen's book "Beat The Relationship Odds" gives you an insightful look into the dynamics and sometimes complicated world of marriage and relationships. Margaret uses easy to understand analogies and her processes and tools will help and benefit any relationship. Having been married for over 39 years myself, I highly recommend Margaret's book to anyone that would like to enhance their present relationships or to lay a foundation that will allow them to create the relationship that they have always wanted."

— **Gary Barnes,** American's Traction Coach
www.GaryBarnesInternational.com

"Beat The Relationship Odds is a comprehensive, insightful book designed to help the thoughtful reader enhance his life and become the best he can be. Ms. Johansen has involved herself in the cutting-edge brain research of today, and has translated that difficult technical information into language everyone can understand and utilize. She outlines the step-by-step process of observing one's emotions and regulating one's responses to enable the reader to create relationships they want and deserve.

I highly recommend this well written book to all readers interested in improving their quality of life, enhancing their communication skills, and deepening their relationships. I laud Ms. Johansen for her ingenious ability to engage the reader with germane stories, pertinent exercises, and down to earth wisdom. This book is a great read!"

> — **Christy Monson**, MA, MFT, Author of *Becoming Free: A Woman's Guide to Internal Strength. And, Love, Hugs, and Hope When Scary Things Happen*

"WOW!!! This book is life-changing and should be read by everyone! If you're ready to have a stronger, deeper relationship, then read and absorb the strategies in this brilliant book by my friend, Margaret Johansen!"

> — **James Malinchak,**
> featured on ABCs hit TV show, *Secret Millionaire*, Founder, www.BigMoneySpeaker.com

"We always hear 'relationships take work'...
but Margaret Johansen shows us how to put
the 'play' back in them instead. She honed
her technique through years of working
with real-life couples, and this book is clear,
simple and brilliant. It's a must-read for anyone
who wants to learn how to create and keep the relationship
of their dreams!"

— **Barbara Niven**
  Actress, Media Trainer, Speaker & Author
  www.BarbaraNiven.com

"When I met my future wife, I had no idea the months
following would present challenges neither of us had ever
faced. But, after a severe fall, a car accident, two brain
injuries, and two surgeries, this is what we faced. Although
there continues to be challenges, when we learned the
strategies within this book, it really helped us see things
through a different lens, especially the analogy of
rattlesnakes, squirrels, and elephants that live in our brain!
For any couple who deals with challenges (which I suppose
is ALL of us), we both highly recommend the amazing
knowledge, unique perspective and simple delivery of a
complex topic. It will hugely help you!!"

— **TW Walker,** Author, Superhero Success
  www.SuperheroSuccess.com

"An absolute 'must read' for everyone interested in how and why some people can work
and live together harmoniously ...and why
some can't...and that should include all of us.

Reading this book will take you on a fascinating
journey of self-discovery and provide you with the power to
influence yourself and others with unprecedented

impact and precision. If your goal is to become a better
communicator with your spouse and improve family
relationships this is the book to read. Additionally, this book
offers a much needed guide to understanding people and
their behaviors."

— **Donald C. Kauffman, MA**
    Organizational Development Coach
    Kauffman Group Consulting President

"Words cannot describe the overall benefit I have received
from Margaret. Her essence has taught me calm. Her
common sense has brought guidance that now permeates
each day of my life. Her grace and wisdom has helped me
restore self-acceptance in a profound way. How do you 'pay'
someone for this? I try to pass it on to others now."

— **DD,** Author

"Warm. Compassionate. Understanding. Insightful. Solution-
oriented. The quality of her work is genius."

— **RG,** Real Estate Investor, Executive Management

"Warm and believable, with a lively brilliance and sense of humor, Margaret creates a compelling presence. Her ability to be with people as they are in great pain amazes me, because she never looses her humanity and compassion for suffering. Yet, along with this is a keen intellect that is incisive, as she helps me see clearly the mask I am wearing. She provides a credible bridge between logic and faith by articulately presenting bits and pieces of research and cutting-edge findings that help explain why I am the way I am and how, then, I can change, always supportive and caring in how she does this. I don't understand, really, how she gets me to strive for more excellence and responsibility, but she does. It's amazingly helpful and life-changing."

— **SW**, Professional Athlete

"The things my husband and I appreciate about Margaret are: she never takes sides, but speaks to both of us directly with respect and kindness; there is always a sense of peace in her work; the homework assignments greatly help each of us better understand ourselves and also improves our ability to relate to how the other person thinks. Our marriage is much better from her assistance and wonderful spirit."

— **J/JR**, Married Couple

"Such a huge help — my husband and I learned so much. We never would have made it without her."

— **SP**, Homemaker, Las Vegas

"To be in Margaret's presence is calming, clarifying, and allows the mental mind to just be quiet. There is never any attack, just really good questions that cause me to think -- and to think in ways that are new areas of exploration for me. Margaret's breadth of knowledge is impressive. But, the wisdom and general understanding of Life that comes through her work reflects a spiritual IQ that is off the charts. The help I have received with her guidance is indescribable."

— **JD**, CEO Business Executive

38065412R00086

Made in the USA
Middletown, DE
12 December 2016